BOB CHANDLER'S
TALES FROM THE
SAN DIEGO PADRES
DUGOUT

BOB CHANDLER'S
TALES FROM THE
SAN DIEGO PADRES
DUGOUT

A COLLECTION OF THE GREATEST PADRES STORIES EVER TOLD

BOB CHANDLER
WITH BILL SWANK
FOREWORD BY JERRY COLEMAN

**SPORTS
PUBLISHING**

Sports Publishing books may be purchased in bulk at special discounts for sales promotion, corporate gifts, fund-raising, or educational purposes. Special editions can also be created to specifications. For details, contact the Special Sales Department, Sports Publishing, 307 West 36th Street, 11th Floor, New York, NY 10018 or sportspubbooks@skyhorsepublishing.com.

Sports Publishing® is a registered trademark of Skyhorse Publishing, Inc.®, a Delaware corporation.

Visit our website at www.sportspubbooks.com

10 9 8 7 6 5 4 3 2

Library of Congress Cataloging-in-Publication Data is available on file.

ISBN: 978-1-68358-372-1
eBook ISBN: 978-1-61321-307-0

Series design by Tom Lau
Jacket photograph: Getty Images

Printed in China

For my family, who endured over 30 years of my major league baseball travel, encompassing roughly four months each season. Fortunately, they were able to share some of the travel and some of the tales. I think they enjoyed the time in Yuma the most— after all, I spent cumulatively about two years at the Padres first spring training site.

—B.C.

Contents

Foreword ix

Acknowledgments xi

Introduction xiii

Chapter 1: Is 2020 Finally the Year? 1

Chapter 2: A Franchise Is Born 11

Chapter 3: From Jose Arcia
        to Ozzie Smith 16

Chapter 4: The Good, the Bad,
        and the Ugly 24

Chapter 5: Early Padres Stars 36

Chapter 6: Broadcasting 54

Chapter 7: Ray Kroc 71

Chapter 8: Spring Training 78

Chapter 9: Hang a Star on 1984 86

Chapter 10: Three Frustrating
        Seasons 105

Chapter 11: The Most Exciting Season
      in Franchise History 115

Chapter 12: The Best Season—1998........ 125

Chapter 13: Potpourri.................................... 140

Chapter 14: On the Road 152

Chapter 15: Characters................................. 157

Chapter 16: Tony Gwynn
      Bits and Pieces....................................... 170

Epilogue.. 178

foreword

Jerry Coleman was one of the finest men I have ever known and a great friend. He wrote this forward for the 2006 first issue of the book just one year after entering the broadcasting wing of the National Baseball Hall of Fame. Jerry played all or part of nine seasons with the New York Yankees winning six world series including five in a row from 1949 through 1953 as a second baseman. He was also a Marine fighter pilot who served in both the Second World War and Korean War. We began together as the Padres radio-tv broadcasting team starting with the 1972 season. Jerry was selected for the Padres Hall of Fame in 2012 when the team erected a statue in his honor at Petco Park. He was still working as a club broadcaster when he passed away in January, 2014 at the age of 89.

The story of the San Diego Padres started in 1969, and Bob Chandler was there. In fact, he is the one person in San Diego most qualified to bring the entire Padres story to the surface.

Bob began as a TV sportscaster in San Diego, worked over 30 years as one of the radio/TV voices of the Padres and even spent several years handling the team's public relations.

My association with Bob began in 1972, when the two of us became the new radio/TV voices of the team. We experienced many lean years on the field and at the gate until Ray Kroc came on the scene in 1974. The club began to show improvement as Kroc spent millions of dollars on free agents and tried to upgrade the organization. We enjoyed the fruitful Randy Jones years and the arrival of Dave Winfield and Tony Gwynn.

Finally, in the 10th year of the franchise, the team had a winning record in 1978. Six years later, we all shared the joy of winning the National League pennant and going to the World Series. Through the lean times and the good times, Bob was the ultimate professional on the air and a great friend away from the ballpark. There is no telling how many meals we shared over the years, solving all of the Padres'—and baseball's—problems.

Several other announcers joined us during the last four decades, most notably Dave Campbell, Rick Monday, and Ted Leitner. Leitner used to refer to Bob as the "B-C-P-C" (Bob Chandler, Personal Computer), because of his ability to remember facts, figures, and stories and tell them on the air.

Bob tells about the importance of having a broadcast partner in the booth during the late innings at Wrigley Field. Did I really have that much difficulty pronouncing the last name of a certain Phillies Hall of Fame third baseman? I had great fun reminiscing about the time Ray Kroc took the microphone at the stadium. Of course, Bob remembers every detail of that memorable night.

What great times and great stories! They are all in his *Tales from the San Diego Padres*. I hope you readers enjoy the "tales" as much as we enjoyed living them.

I hang a star on your book, Bob.

Your Friend,

Jerry Coleman

Bob Chandler (left), Jerry Coleman (foreground), and Tommy Jorgensen (back). From the Bob Chandler collection

Acknowledgments

The title of this book is *Bob Chandler's Tales from the San Diego Padres*. Although most of the tales are mine, trust me when I say my partner Bill Swank deserves equal billing. I am a rookie author. Swank has published several books, and he is San Diego's top baseball historian. Bill helped guide me through the rough spots and smooth out my style of writing. Even though Swank helped edit my copy, the content is my responsibility.

Thanks to our friends at the San Diego Hall of Champions and San Diego Padres for their photographs. People love pictures, and photographers never receive enough credit for their work.

We have been fortunate to have an energetic young editor, Travis Moran, who understands baseball. We call him "Trevor" Moran because he is a great closer. He's been our bullpen ace back in Illinois.

My experience with the Padres goes back to the Pacific Coast League days and many of the "tales" were stored in my memory. We did our best to double-check facts. If there are any errors, we take full responsibility. I started from scratch in writing this book and almost every day would remember another story.

In that respect, the book turned into a labor of love as I recalled many of the fun and frustrating times of Padres baseball. In some way, I am indebted to all the front office people, managers, coaches, players, broadcasters, and writers connected with the San Diego Padres since the franchise was awarded to my favorite city on May 27, 1968.

In mid October 2005, I played golf with one-time Padres manager Roger Craig. Craig began his major league career in 1955, a full half-century ago, with the Brooklyn Dodgers. Roger remarked to my other golfing partners, Bob Skinner and Norm Sherry, how quickly the 50 years have passed . . . that it didn't really seem that long ago they were all playing major league baseball. I feel the same way about covering and broadcasting the San Diego Padres. It's been a terrific ride.

Bob Chandler

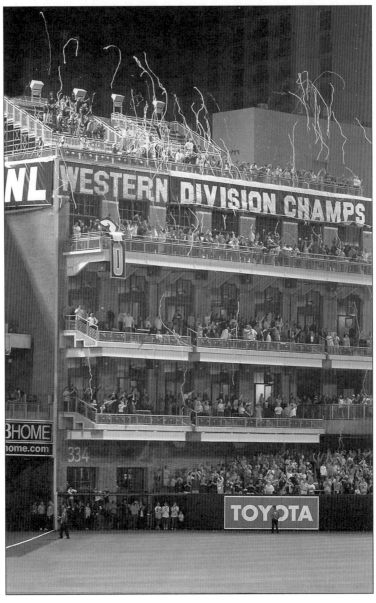

Padres Clinch Western Division Pennant—September 28, 2005.
from the San Diego Padres; Chris Hardy, team photographer

Introduction

In baseball and in life, timing is everything. When opportunity suddenly appears as big as a watermelon over home plate, you swing for the fences.

Dion Rich is the World's Greatest Gate Crasher, the King of Barter, and the founding patriarch of Family Tickets Service, which is everything the name implies. The Greatest also hosts a spontaneous floating lunch group for gray and graying (bald and balding) sportsmen, usually on a Thursday or Friday, whenever he can arrange a tradeout meal at one of San Diego's finest restaurants. Dion begins calling friends on his Rolodex around 10:00 a.m., inviting them to meet at noon. If the timing is right, you get a free lunch, and a true sportsman would never pass up a free meal.

At one of these impromptu get-togethers in early April 2005, Dion introduced us to his new tradeout lawyer, David Ortega, Esquire, who was properly impressed with his tablemates. He was even impressed with me and said, "Nobody knows more about baseball in San Diego than you."

Though flattered, modesty forced me to demur. "You can't say that with Bob Chandler sitting right across from me. Nobody knows more about the big league Padres than Bob Chandler except for Jerry Coleman . . . and Jerry has probably forgotten most of what he knows."

Attorney Ortega exchanged similar greetings with Bob and former NFL defensive coach and poet, Tom Bass. Bob and Tom are old friends in the sports broadcasting business. We stayed late, swapped stories, and because the timing was right, I began to work on Bob about writing this book. He was typically polite but noncommittal.

In May, we met for breakfast at Albie's in Mission Valley. Finally, with a grin, Bob agreed to do the book. Since then, he has been fully focused on bringing you almost 40 years of his favorite tales from the Padres. Remember that when this team was bad, which was often, it was horrible. Through it all, Bob Chandler remained optimistic and positive. He reflects with humor on the lean years and with pride in the glory years.

We have all enjoyed his casual, but consistently professional, approach to the game on television and radio. I have now witnessed, up close, his love for baseball and for the Padres. San Diego was picked to win the NL West in 2005. Bob agreed they would take the West, but I thought these Padres were, at best, a .500 team. I'll never forget an early August 2005 e-mail from Bob when the team slipped below .500 and into a first-place tie with the Arizona Diamondbacks. Succinctly he wrote, "We both appear to be wrong."

As we know, the Padres persevered and eventually claimed the NL West with an 82-80 record, although it took Trevor Hoffman's 436th career save to seal victory over their rival Dodgers to avoid a .500 season.

In closing, Bob Chandler truly is a fine gentleman. Mention his name, and people always say, "I like Bob Chandler."

You will enjoy his memories. . . .

And, by the way, thanks for lunch, Dion. This book would not have happened without you. You are a man who understands the importance of timing.

And thanks to the Padres—your timing was pretty good this year, too.

Chapter 1

Is 2020 Finally the Year?

In 2010, the San Diego Padres challenged for the NL West title, but lost it to the San Francisco Giants on the final day of the regular season. Since then, the Padres have had nine-straight losing seasons, matching the futility of the first nine years of the team's existence (1969-1977).

In 2020, the Padres hired a new manager, Jayce Tingler, are returning the team colors to their original brown, and are planning on a winning season with the hope of contending for a playoff spot. Here's why.

In 2016, the Padres embarked on a five-year rebuilding plan. They traded away veteran players for prospects, invested roughly $80 million in young international talent, and tried to take advantage of high draft picks. It was a similar strategy as that employed by the Houston Astros and Chicago Cubs, who both have won the World Series in recent seasons.

Houston started it's re-build in 2011, losing 106, 107, and 111 games those first three years. In 2014, they improved to 70-92 and in the fifth year finally had a winning season at 86-76. Two years later, in 2017, the Astros went 101-61 and captured the World Series crown.

The Chicago Cubs began their rebuild in 2011 and lost 91, 101, 96 and 89 games those first four seasons. In year five they jumped to 97-65 and in 2016 won the World Series after a 103-58 regular season.

The Padres have lost 94, 91, 96, and 90 games in those first four years of their rebuild and now hope to emulate the Astros and Cubs with a winning season in year five.

Do they have the talent, and is it battle tested? For the last three years, various baseball rating services have judged the Padres to have the league's best farm system, and some of those prospects are starting to join the Padres. Two of the best are shortstop Fernando Tatis, Jr. and pitcher Chris Paddack.

During the rebuild, the Padres also invested millions of dollars in free agent first baseman Eric Hosmer and third baseman Manny Machado.

Critics point out Padres general manager A. J. Preller has shown he can develop a productive farm system, but hasn't shown he can put together a contending major league team. Probably a fair criticism, underlining why 2020 is such a pivotal year for the Padres and Preller.

Depending on when you read this, you'll know what the goal is and whether or not it was achieved.

Tatis, Jr. and Paddack

The Padres first year of the major rebuild was 2016, and two trades the team made in June of that year figure to be major building blocks.

On June 4, the Padres sent veteran right-handed pitcher James Shields and a big chunk of his salary to the Chicago White Sox for pitcher Erik Johnson and a 17-year-old infielder named Fernando Tatis, Jr. The White Sox felt they had a chance to make the playoffs in 2016, and thought a veteran pitcher like Shields could help them make a run. The Padres asked for several different Chicago prospects, but were turned down.

Padres pro scouting director Pete DeYoung and scout Spencer Graham decided to check out some of the younger White Sox prospects training in Phoenix, Arizona, during instructional camp which traditionally takes place between the end of spring training and the start of rookie league ball in June. They were struck by the tools of the young Tatis, and suggested other Padre scouts to check him out. Other baseball personnel—including vice president/assistant general manager Fred Uhlman—validated their scouting reports and the

White Sox agreed to trade the 17-year-old, plus the veteran pitcher Erik Johnson, for Shields.

It should be noted that only a small percentage of 17-year-old prospects ever make it to the majors, but the Padres were early in their rebuilding process and decided to take a chance. Johnson had arm issues and never worked out, but, in 2019, Tatis exploded onto the major league scene.

How good can Tatis be? In my opinion, he has the tools, talent, and makeup to become a generational player for the Padres. In 1988, Roberto Alomar broke in with the Padres and made an immediate impact in what would become a Hall of Fame career.

In spring training 2019, I first witnessed Tatis playing in exhibition games. I was stunned to see he had more range than Alomar, a better arm, was a faster runner, had lots more power, and was a better hitter. He had just turned 20 on January 2, 1999.

In slightly more than half a season, Tatis batted .317 with 22 homers, 53 RBIs, and 16 stolen bases (while finishing third in the NL Rookie of the Year voting). Double those numbers and you have a generational player. Alex Rodriguez is the last shortstop to put up numbers like this at that age.

Tatis plays the game with such joy that he inspires other players around him, and his instincts for the game make him a fun player to watch—even if he's not on your team. If there is one caution, it's the fact both his 2018 and 2019 seasons ended early because of injuries.

The baseball universe is anxious to see what comes next.

On June 30, 2016, the Padres made a similar deal with the Miami Marlins. Padres closer Fernando Rodney was having an excellent season in San Diego, and the Marlins, like the White Sox, felt he could help them reach the playoffs.

Scouts Dave Post and Steve Lyons spotted a tall Texan named Chris Paddack pitching for the Marlins low Class-A team in Greensboro, North Carolina. Paddack was 20 at the time, and Padre scouts were impressed with his fastball, change up, and command at that young age. The 6-4 Texan did not have a real curve ball and the Marlins projected Paddack as maybe a one-inning reliever. Thus, they agreed to trade him to the Padres for Rodney.

Paddack was moved to the Padres low Class-A team in Fort Wayne and made an immediate impression, allowing just one run in 14 innings with 23 strikeouts. Unfortunately, he also came down with a bad elbow and had to undergo Tommy John surgery, which wiped out his 2017 season.

What happened next left quite an impression with the Padres baseball brain trust. Paddack came to San Diego and vowed to club brass that he would work his tail off and prove to San Diego they made a good deal.

In 2018, Paddack turned in impressive numbers at high Single-A Lake Elsinore and Double-A San Antonio.

In 2019, Paddack earned a spot in the Padres rotation at spring training and, despite limitations on his innings pitched, turned in a very good season. In 141 innings, he was 9-7 with a 3.33 ERA, allowing just 107 hits while striking out 153 (averaging 9.8 strikeouts a game). He also began to develop a breaking pitch.

There will be no pitching restrictions on the young Texan in 2020, and the Padres expect him to be a key member of their starting rotation.

June 2016 could turn out to be a historic month in the Padres future.

Jayce Tingler

How much pressure is on new Padres manager Jayce Tingler as he begins the first season of a three-year contract in 2020? Padres executive chairman Ron Fowler pointed out that 2020 is the fifth year of the team's rebuild and he expects winning baseball. "The Padres sucked after the All-Star Game in 2019, winning only 35 percent of their games," Fowler said. "That's unacceptable. We've got to win— and we've got to win now."

Is Tingler equipped to do that? What's his background?

Tingler was a 10th-round draft pick of the Toronto Blue Jays in 2003. Two years later, he was taken in the minor league Rule 5 draft by the Texas Rangers. The man who chose him was A. J. Preller, currently the Padres GM and the same person who chose him now to lead his team on the field. During his tenure with the Rangers, Tingler worked in the front office, in development, as a major league coach, and manager of various minor league teams in the club's system.

Despite no major league managerial experience, he comes highly recommended by various baseball people.

Current Padres broadcaster Tony Gwynn, Jr. knows Tingler from their playing days in the Cape Cod summer league. Tony said Tingler has a good baseball mind and was constantly talking baseball and actually offered Gwynn a coaching job in the Texas organization. Former Padres outfielder Will Venable was traded to Texas and remembers, "Tingler had the ear of the players and their respect. When he spoke, you knew he knew what he was talking about."

Rangers broadcaster Eric Nadel, current manager Chris Woodward, and team president Jon Daniels all sung his praises, emphasizing his energy, preparation, and communication skills. Tingler also played summer ball in Missouri with future first-ballot Hall of Famer Albert Pujols, who took the time to contact Padres personnel and praise the decision to hire him as manager.

What does all this mean? It's nice, but I've learned over 40 years in the baseball business you never know what kind of manager a person will be until he does it.

In baseball, most people have opinions on who they think will be a good manager. Some succeed, while others don't work out. A personal example is probably future Hall of Fame manager Bruce Bochy. I first met Bruce in the mid-80s as a backup catcher for the Padres. A good guy, popular with his teammates, and a practical joker in the clubhouse. I never thought of Bochy as a future major league skipper. After he retired, the Padres gave him a chance to manage in the lower minors. He was successful at every rung of the ladder, and eventually took over the major league team and guided the Padres to the 1998 World Series. After three World Series championships with the San Francisco Giants, Bochy now appears a lock for the Hall of Fame.

Just for the record, 8 of the 10 teams in the 2019 postseason were guided by first-time managers.

Padres Return to Brown Uniforms in 2020

When the major league Padres first took the field in 1969, their uniforms were light beige with brown hats. Many people thought the color was a tribute to Father Junipero Serra, who founded California's first mission in San Diego.

Franciscan Padres still wear brown habits and the Padres will return to brown in 2020, but the color never had any connection with the religious order.

The fact is, Padres first owner C. Arnholt Smith simply liked the color brown. Some would say he had a brown fetish. Daily, he would wear brown suits with brown shirts, ties, and shoes. Even the team's news releases were printed in brown ink.

Franciscan brown is a good story. It makes perfect sense for the Padres to wear brown, but it just didn't happen that way.

After Tony Gwynn was drafted by the club in 1981, his first reaction was, "Aw (bleep), the Padres. That damn brown and gold." Sartorially splendid Steve Garvey also hated the brown uniforms, complaining, "The Padres uniform makes me look like a taco." Kurt Bevacqua was typically more graphic. "We look like nine piles of manure in a cow pasture."

In the mid-80s, the Padres switched their primary uniform color to blue.

But Tony Gwynn grew nostalgic and had a change of heart. When asked about a possible return to brown, he said, "I'd love it. That's how we started, with brown. I'd love to see brown." Not everybody likes the idea, but the Padres will be back in brown for 2020.

After all, the first Padre player was Brown. Outfielder Ollie Brown was selected number one by the club in the expansion draft to stock the 1969 team.

2011 Through 2019

When this book was originally published in 2006, the Padres had won the 2005 National League West. A paperback edition was released the following year after they repeated as 2006 NL West champions. Jake Peavy received all 32 first-place votes to win the 2007 Cy Young Award. The club's 2004 move to play downtown in beautiful Petco Park offered great promise for the future.

The book was again updated in 2012, with the Padres seemingly under new ownership. Hope remained high. The team had won 90 games in 2010 to finish a surprising second in the league. Bud Black was selected as the National League Manager of the Year.

Young Padres ace Jake Peavy.
From the San Diego Padres; Chris Hardy, team photographer

The 2011 season proved to be a difficult one for the Padres. Rather than keep Adrian Gonzalez for the last year off his contract, he was traded to the Boston Red Sox. The Padres finished last in the NL West (71-91) and, without Gonzalez's potent bat, were last in home runs (91), fewest runs scored (593), and their team .237 batting average was next to last in MLB.

If the team wouldn't pay to retain their stars, the future appeared problematic.

2012

Before the start of the 2012 season, the deal for former player-agent Jeff Moored to purchase the Padres from John Moores fell though. An anonymous MLB source said, "We've had so many crazy things go on in baseball at the ownership level last year with the Mets and the Dodgers and the Astros—but what's happened with the Padres is the most intriguing."

Another MLB insider noted, "Jeff started off in a bad situation with the Padres because he had people in the game who didn't like him and they were looking for any reason to justify him not getting the [owners] vote."

On the field, the club started the season 20-41, but played over .500 ball the rest of the way and improved to 76-86, finishing in fourth place. Third baseman Chase Headley had a breakout year; he was the National League Player of the Month for August and September. Headley exploded for 31 home runs and led the National League with 115 RBIs. Shortstop Everth Cabrera stole the league-high 44 bases. Workhorse Clayton Richard was the top pitcher, with a 14-14 record.

2013

The Padres repeated their 76-86 record to tie for third place with the defending World Series champion San Francisco Giants in the NL West. Rookie second baseman Jedd Gyorko showed promise with his bat, and newcomer Andrew Cashner went 10-9 with a 3.09 ERA. Were the Padres on the verge of breaking even?

2014

San Diego did improve in 2014 . . . but barely. They finished 77-85, with the league's lowest team batting average (.226), 12 percentage points below Cincinnati (.238). One positive was that the pitching staff (including Ian Kennedy, Tyson Ross, Eric Stults, and Huston Street) posted the second-lowest ERA (3.27) in the National League.

2015

There was a major shakeup in 2015. New general manager A. J. Preller attempted to turn the Padres into an instant pennant contender. He traded away seven of the team's top eleven farm hands, including Trea Turner to get Wil Myers, Matt Kemp, and the Upton brothers (Justin and Melvin). They failed to produce, but newly acquired closer Craig Kimbrel saved 39 games and free agent pitcher James Shields went 13-7.

The Padres were 32-33 in June, so manager Bud Black was fired. Bud wasn't the problem. Through nine seasons with the club, Black had only two winning seasons (2007 and 2010), and finished with an overall record of 649-713 (.477 winning percentage). After firing Black, the Padres tumbled to fourth place with a 74-88 record. Current Dodgers manager Dave Roberts was a coach on the team and managed for one game until former collegiate coach and Padres minor league manager Pat Murphy took over the helm. Another minor league manager in the Padres system, Andy Green, was given the job for 2016. His future would be bleak.

Was Andy Green a Bad Manager?

Put another way, was Andy Green given a chance to be a good manager? In his first year (2016), the Padres opened the season with three game against the Dodgers and failed to score a run. They would be shut out in five of their first ten games. Was that Green's fault?

For five of the previous six years—2014-2019—the Padres finished last in National League batting. In 2018, they hit .235, one percentage point above the worst in the league.

Before 2019, the last Padre to hit over .300 for a season was Brian Giles in 2008 (.306). Since 2012, the leading hitters were: Chris Denorfia (.293 in 2012), Everth Cabrera (.283 in 2013), Seth Smith (.266 in 2014), Yonder Alonso (.282 in 2015), Jon Jay (.291 in 2016), Jose Pirela (.288 in 2017) and, Travis Jankowski (.259 in 2018).

In 2012, the Padres finished 8th in the National League in team strikeouts and progressively got worse. They were 12th in 2013, 10th in 2014, 13th in 2015, 14th (next to last) in both 2016 and 2017, and 15th (last) in both 2018 and 2019.

The 2019 Houston Astros set an unusual MLB record for strikeouts: most strikeouts thrown by pitchers (1,671) and fewest strikeouts by batters (1,166). It was the first time that the same team finished first in each category.

The 2019 Padres batters ranked #29 (last) with 1,581 strikeouts. Put another way, the Astros struck out 18.7 percent of the time and the Padres stuck out 26.3 percent of the time. Statistically, every fourth Padres batter struck out. As a team, they struck out 9.76 times a game.

Since the move to Petco Park in 2004, the Padres have gone through ten different hitting coaches: Dave Magadan, Merv Rettenmund, Wally Joyner, Jim Lefebvre, Randy Ready, Phil Plantier, Mark Kotsay, Alan Zinter, Matt Stairs, and Johnny Washington. Batting coach for the San Diego Padres must be the most difficult job in baseball.

Was the continued bad hitting Green's fault?

Every year since 2015, San Diego's pitching staff has been in the bottom third of the National League. In 2019, they were 12th with a 4.60 ERA. It is not easy to compete in the major leagues with young pitchers and limited pitch restrictions. Was that Green's fault?

It appeared the Padres had turned the corner in 2019, and were 45-45 at the All-Star break. Then the wheels fell off and they finished with a 70-92 record. Andy Green was fired with eight games remaining in the season but, in fairness, he never had the opportunity to manage a major league roster. Maybe he never should have been a big-league manager in the first place.

The 2020 season will determine if blame should be placed higher in the organization.

Chapter 2

A Franchise Is Born

It Was May 27, 1968

I
t was May 27, 1968. I was preparing for my evening sportscast as the sports director at Channel 39, which then used the call letters KCST. All of a sudden, bells indicated that a bulletin was coming across the UPI Wire Machine. I excitedly read: "Dateline—Chicago (UPI)—The National League voted Monday night to expand to 12 teams, adding San Diego and Montreal for the 1969 season."

Major League Baseball was officially born in San Diego.

Ironically, I'd first fallen in love with the game almost 20 years to the day. In 1948, my dad was a naval officer stationed in Washington, D.C. On May 28 of that year, he took me to Griffith Stadium in Washington to watch the original Senators host the Boston Red Sox. To this day, I remember Washington won 2-1. Eddie Yost of the Senators hit a triple, and Stan Spence of Boston popped up to end the game with the bases loaded.

However, mostly I remember my dad telling me that #9 for Boston was the greatest hitter in baseball. I was 10 years old and couldn't believe I was in the same hemisphere with baseball's best hitter. I immediately became a big fan of Ted Williams, not having any idea that he was from San Diego, and I would eventually have a chance to meet him.

As a side note, my eventual play-by-play partner, Jerry Coleman, told me just how awful those old Washington teams were. He said if the Yankees didn't win 20 of the 22-game season series, they considered it an off year. Nevertheless, in the late 1940s and early 1950s, I lived and died with the likes of Al Evans, Mickey Vernon, Al Kozar, Sam Dente, Carden Gillenwater, Gil Coan, Eddie Stewart, and many other long forgotten ballplayers.

I Was Planning to Become a Baseball Announcer

Coming from a Navy family, we moved every few years to a different locale: from Washington to San Diego to Pearl Harbor to Newport, Rhode Island. In fact, my high school career began in 1952 at San Diego High, continued at Roosevelt High in Honolulu, followed by graduation at Rogers High School in Newport, where in 1955 I decided I wanted to go to college at San Diego State. I began as an SDSC freshman in the fall of 1956, and I've been a resident ever since. Actually, I was born in San Diego's Mercy Hospital in 1937, when my Dad was stationed aboard a destroyer docked at North Island.

In the back of my mind, I was planning to become a baseball announcer, but not until I had first finished my career as a major league ballplayer. It took about 10 minutes on the practice field at San Diego State to realize the quality of baseball in Southern California was light years ahead of the ball I had been playing in Rhode Island. At that point, I decided to prepare for what I hoped would become my career announcing baseball.

During my four and a half years on the Aztec campus, I took a tape recorder out to the SDSC baseball games, sat in the stands, and endured catcalls and abuse as I tried my hand at play-by-play. After each game, I would take my tape to baseball coach Charlie Smith, and he would critique it. Fortunately, none of those tapes remains in existence.

I also broadcast some San Diego State basketball and football games over the San Diego Junior College radio station, KSDS, which had a working agreement with SDSC since the four-year school had no radio station of its own.

The Aztec football program was in the pre-Don Coryell years, and the teams were not very good. You could say it helped prepare me for broadcasting some of the Padre teams in future years.

One San Diego State-Fresno State football game still bothers me. On a warm homecoming Saturday afternoon at Aztec Bowl, Fresno State was so far ahead at halftime that their players just lounged in the end zone and watched the homecoming floats pass in review. I thought that was the ultimate insult!

A Paid Sportscasting Gig

My last two years at San Diego State, I actually got a paid sports-casting job. I was hired for $10 a game to broadcast the "High School Football Game of the Week in the Grossmont High School District over KUFM-FM, the voice of the foothills in El Cajon." I was thrilled as I recruited some fraternity brothers to spot and keep statistics for me. Most of the games were broadcast from a stadium near El Cajon Speedway. (I use the term stadium very loosely.)

My first real job was at Channel 8, working as a newsreel cameraman-writer, which was actually great training, and to this day, I still use some of the fundamentals I learned there. Sports were still my ambition, and I won an audition to do the weekend sports broadcast. My competition was one other person who applied for the job. Once again, the extra pay was only $10 per show. However, after one month in March 1962, there was a union problem, and KFMB decided to have one person do both sports and weather. My career stalled as I returned to my full-time newsreel duties.

Al Couppee

In March 1963, I got my first real chance in sports. Al Couppee, the sports director of Channel 10, hired me as his assistant. We became the first two-person sportscasting department in San Diego. Of course, Channel 8 and Channel 6 were the only other TV stations operating in San Diego at that time. Channel 10 was owned by Time-Life Broadcast and changed the call letters of both their TV and radio stations from KFSD to KOGO. They even had a guy dressed in a kangaroo outfit who made personal appearances as the KOGOROO—it was great publicity.

While working for Couppee, I wrote and produced his two daily TV sportscasts and his five-minute radio sportscast. I also handled the

(left to right) My Channel 10 KOGO-TV buddy Al Couppee, pro-golfer Billy Casper, and me. From the Bob Chandler collection

talent on the four weekend sports telecasts and had the opportunity to do play-by-play of high school football on radio.

Part of my job was to film segments for Couppee's weekly half-hour *Outdoor Sportsman* show. My first week, he invited me to go on an early-morning sportfishing trip. I had just been hired and didn't think it was a good idea to tell him that I was prone to seasickness. We met at four in the morning, and by the time the boat reached the bait tank, I was already leaning over the side. The rest of the day was spent filming and using the bucket at my side. I got the job done, but Coup never invited me to go sportfishing again.

Channel 39 KCST-TV

In 1968, I left Channel 10 to become sports director of a new UHF Station, Channel 39 KCST-TV. There was no cable TV in 1968. Television sets had to have a special antenna to receive the UHF signal. Only about one-third of the sets in San Diego could even get the station, and the new owners, Bass Brothers Broadcasting of Dallas, Texas, decided to lure viewers by programming massive local sports coverage.

I was like a kid in a candy store. In addition to a one-hour nightly sportscast, I had a chance to do play-by-play of Padres baseball, San Diego Chargers football (including *The Sid Gillman Show* and a highlight show), San Diego State football, basketball, baseball, rugby, and track and field, plus high school basketball and various assorted other events like golf and military sports. Some of the major sports events we televised attracted a good audience, and it's fair to say many sports fans found it necessary to learn how to receive UHF.

What I didn't know was the planned strategy of Bass Brothers Broadcasting. They wanted to increase their audience to show the FCC they were a viable TV station in the San Diego market. Thus the ABC Network, which was carried on Mexican station XETV, had to move to KCST. After a lengthy court battle, that's exactly what happened. Then ABC made a deal with Channel 10, and the NBC network moved from Channel 10 to Channel 39, which is the arrangement that exists today.

I Achieved My Dream

For me, my Padre telecasts on Channel 39 opened the door to join the Padres as one of their full-time broadcasters. I joined Jerry Coleman as the new broadcast team at the start of the 1972 season. It took 11 years of working in the market, but finally I achieved my dream of broadcasting major league baseball in my hometown of San Diego.

Chapter 3

From Jose Arcia to Ozzie Smith

The Golden Decade of Sports in San Diego

A s a young sportscaster just beginning my career in 1961, I was involved in all of the various sports activities, and it was an exciting time. The golden decade of sports in San Diego was the 1960s. Consider this: In 1961, the Chargers moved from Los Angeles to San Diego, providing the city with its first major league sports franchise. The early Chargers were one of professional football's most exciting teams with offensive genius Sid Gillman as general manager-head coach. Players like Lance Alworth, John Hadl, Keith Lincoln, Paul Lowe, Ron Mix, Walt Sweeney, Ernie Ladd, and Earl Faison helped establish the game in San Diego. Don Coryell's highly successful tenure as head football coach at San Diego State also began in '61. In 1960, the Aztecs had a miserable 1-6-1 record. The following year, San Diego State went 7-2-1—Coryell's worst season over the next 10 years. In November 1965, over 72 percent of San Diego voters cast ballots in favor of building a multipurpose stadium in Mission Valley.

In November 1966, a new sports arena opened with the Western Hockey League San Diego Gulls hosting the Seattle Totems before a sellout crowd of 11,692. The WHL was one of professional hockey's top minor leagues, with teams in Los Angeles and San Francisco. In 1967, San Diego Stadium opened with an exhibition game between the Chargers and the NFL's Detroit Lions. A merger had been agreed upon between the upstart AFL and the longtime NFL, but full consolidation had not yet taken place. Thus, it was a big deal for the Chargers to host an NFL team. Since San Diego had a new sports arena, the NBA expanded to San Diego, and the Rockets began play in October 1967.

Finally, to cap off the greatest decade in San Diego sports history, the National League expanded to San Diego, and the Padres began play in San Diego Stadium in 1969.

Trading Pitchers for Prospects

The San Diego Padres and Montreal Expos entered the world in 1968, when National League owners voted to expand. In the subsequent draft to stock these teams, the Padres and Expos took opposite approaches. Montreal selected veteran major league players with the idea of trading some of them to other clubs for promising young prospects. The Padres' philosophy was to draft young players and try to build a team for the long run.

How did those philosophies equate into wins that first season of 1969? Both teams had identical and dismal 52-110 records.

For several years after the draft, San Diego tried to build a winning team by trading off their best starting pitchers for two or three prospects, hoping to find solid young players.

Early in the 1969 season, Joe Niekro was acquired along with right-hander Gary Ross and infielder Francisco Libran from the Chicago Cubs in exchange for the Padres' opening-day starter, Dick Selma. Niekro had an overall record of 8-18 with a 3.70 ERA in 221 innings pitched. During the winter, Niekro was swapped to Detroit for pitcher Pat Dobson and infielder Dave Campbell.

Dobson started 34 games for the 1970 Padres, compiling a 14-15 record (3.76) in 251 innings pitched. The Padres needed a shortstop to get rid of the "Arcia Stinks" signs that fans displayed at the stadium. In the off-season, Dobson went to Baltimore for pitcher Tom Phoebus and shortstop Enzo Hernandez—yes, number 11, Enzo Hernandez.

Left-hander Dave Roberts had a terrific season in 1971. In 269 innings pitched, he was 14-17 with a 2.10 earned run average. That could only mean one thing. Roberts's off-season destination was

Houston. Pitcher Bill Greif and infielder Derrel Thomas came to the Padres in return. This futile exercise of trading pitchers for prospects ended as an annual ritual when Ray Kroc took over club ownership in 1974.

A Winning Season

The first nine years of the Padres' existence resulted in nine losing seasons. The Padres averaged over 100 losses during their first six seasons. After the ninth year, their winning percentage improved slightly to .392. If you think it was tough to be a Padres fan during those years, imagine what it was like to broadcast all of those games.

In the Padres' 10th year, the Major League All-Star Game was played in San Diego, but 1978 was important for another reason. The team finally achieved a winning season with an 84-78 record, 11 games out of first place—the closest the Padres had ever come to the division leader as 1,670,107 fans paid to watch the fun. This Padre single-season attendance mark would stand until the pennant-winning year of 1984.

The 1978 season did not give indications of smooth sailing when manager Alvin Dark was fired during spring training. Basically, Padres brass decided Dark's failure to communicate and delegate authority were creating an untenable situation. The coaches were unhappy; the players, on the verge of a revolution, were unhappy; and the media was unhappy. Ray Kroc, who had pushed for the hiring of Dark the previous season, said the firing was actually an easy decision to make.

Padres general manager Bob Fontaine named pitching coach Roger Craig as the interim manager. In his first game at the helm, backup catcher Bob Davis hit a game-winning home run. During the postgame news conference, Fontaine introduced Craig as the interim manager. Obviously flushed with victory, Ray Kroc said, "Take away the interim tag. Craig is our manager. After all, anybody who can turn a .180-hitting catcher into a home-run hitter has to be a great manager."

Craig has always maintained a positive attitude and a sense of perspective. For proof, Roger had a 10-24 record for the 40-120 1962 New York Mets, one of the worst teams in major league history.

When needled about the 24 losses, Craig would respond, "Hey, I won 25 percent of the Mets victories that year."

Indeed, he did . . . 10 of the 40.

Actually, Roger knew a lot about winning. He pitched for the 1955 World Champion Brooklyn Dodgers, the 1959 World Champion Los Angeles Dodgers, and the 1964 World Champion St. Louis Cardinals.

Craig turned out to be an excellent manager for the 1978 Padres, guiding the team to its first winning season ever.

The opening-day lineup looked like this:

1B	**Gene Richards**
2B	**Derrel Thomas**
LF	**Oscar Gamble**
RF	**Dave Winfield**
CF	**George Hendrick**
C	**Gene Tenace**
3B	**Bill Almon**
SS	**Ozzie Smith**
P	**Gaylord Perry**

Ozzie Smith

Ozzie Smith proved to be a brilliant defensive shortstop and was runner-up to Atlanta slugger Bob Horner for 1978 rookie of the year honors. Billy Almon, a one-time No. 1 draft choice of the Padres, had a pretty good rookie season at shortstop in 1977. Meanwhile, Ozzie Smith had played only 68 games of rookie ball when Alvin Dark spotted him in the Arizona Instructional League. Dark had the foresight to immediately appoint Smith as his shortstop. He moved Almon to third base in 1978. Dark certainly could recognize great talent when he saw it. Alvin had been an excellent major league shortstop. He played primarily for the New York Giants. In his college days, the Padres manager was an All-America quarterback at LSU.

I once asked him whether it was tougher to play major college football at quarterback or shortstop in the major leagues.

His answer was succinct.

"Shortstop in the major leagues, because it's every day. Even though I got banged up playing quarterback, I had a whole week to

The wonderful Wizard of Oz (Ozzie Smith) in action as a Padre.
From the San Diego Hall of Champions Collection

rest physically and mentally. In baseball, I had to be physically and mentally ready every game."

Longtime Padres broadcaster and former Yankees infielder Jerry Coleman said he's never seen a better shortstop than Ozzie Smith. Ozzie played in 159 games his rookie year of 1978, batting .258 with 40 stolen bases.

April 20, 1978 marks the date of what became the signature play of Ozzie's career. The Padres were hosting Atlanta in a day game when slugger Jeff Burroughs came to the plate for the Braves. Burroughs hit a sharp ground ball that appeared destined for center field. Ozzie raced to his left and dove for the ball just as it hit something and caromed behind him. While in his dive, Ozzie reached back, and with his bare hand, snagged the baseball.

Smith jumped to his feet and threw Burroughs out on a bang-bang play at first—just one of many sensational plays the great Ozzie Smith made during his Hall of Fame career, and it happened while he was a Padre. Ozzie also regards this as the signature play of his career. Ironically, Jeff Burroughs's son, Sean, would play for the Padres some 25 years later.

Other players who contributed significantly to the Padres' first winning season included Dave Winfield, then in his sixth year with San Diego. Winfield hit .308 with 24 homers, 97 RBIs and 181 hits. Leadoff hitter Gene Richards also batted .308 with 12 triples, 90 runs scored and 37 stolen bases.

Oscar Gamble and Don Lubin

Outfielder Oscar Gamble hit 31 homers for the 1977 Chicago White Sox and became the Padres' marquee off-season position-player acquisition. Don Lubin was Ray Kroc's attorney in Chicago. He strongly recommended to Kroc that the Padres sign Gamble. Baseball people close to the team in 1978 felt Gamble was "psyched out" by the 18-foot outfield walls at San Diego Stadium. He tried to change his swing to upper-cut the ball over the wall, and he ended the season with only seven home runs, a .275 batting average, and 47 RBIs.

The Gamble experiment lasted one year, and then he was traded in the off-season to Texas for first baseman Mike Hargrove. Two years later, Kroc said, "My attorney, Don Lubin, recommended I sign Oscar Gamble. Now the Padres no longer have Gamble—and I no longer have Don Lubin as my attorney."

Jerry Coleman, the Padres' New Skipper

On October 1, 1979, the Padres no longer had Roger Craig as manager. The Moses who led the Padres out of the desert in 1978 was fired after a disappointing 1979 season. Team broadcaster Jerry Coleman was hired as the Padres' new skipper. Because of Jerry's communication skills and ability to deal with people, I thought he would be an excellent manager. However, it had been over 20 years since Coleman had last been in uniform on the field, and he discovered that players' attitudes had changed in the meantime.

Talking baseball with my broadcast partner and new Padres manager, Jerry Coleman, in 1980. From the Bob Chandler collection

Casey Stengel was Jerry's manager with the Yankees, and no player would think of challenging the Old Professor's decisions. They might complain about Stengel's moves, but nobody confronted him. In 1980, players had no qualms about challenging a manager's moves.

I think Coleman had the wrong kind of team for his first managerial effort. The 1980 Padres were primarily a veteran team, pretty much set in their ways. They weren't anxious to adjust to some of Jerry's ideas. Had it been a younger team, Coleman would have had a better chance at success.

The Hot Dog Became Baloney

Retracing the end of the 1979 season, the Padres determined they needed a solid bat to hit behind Dave Winfield. Help was also needed at second base, third base, and center field. General manager Bob Fontaine picked up first baseman Willie Montanez to follow Winfield in the batting order, Dave Cash to play second base, Aurelio Rodriguez at third base, and Jerry Mumphrey to patrol centerfield. Montanez, a hot dog, hit 30 homers in his rookie year for the 1971 Phillies, but his power had turned to baloney by 1980, when he provided just six home runs. Even in spring training, Jerry told me Cash and Rodriguez were over the hill. Only Mumphrey really turned out to be a good acquisition. For the record, Cash batted .227 for the 1980 Padres in what turned out to be his final year in the major leagues. Rodriguez was struggling at .200 after 89 games when the Padres traded him to the New York Yankees. With very little power in his lineup, Coleman tried a running game that set a major league record. Gene Richards, Ozzie Smith, and Jerry Mumphrey became the first threesome to steal 50-plus bases in one season.

"I've Played A Lot of Third Base"

Cash's poor season and the trade of Rodriguez opened the door for a pair of young infielders named Barry Evans and Tim Flannery. Coleman asked Flannery if he had ever played third base.

Flannery lied. "Sure, I've played a lot of third base."

Flannery had never played third base but would do anything to get into the lineup. Flannery hit .240 for the 1980 Padres while Evans finished at .232.

Veteran free-agent pitchers Rick Wise and John Curtis were signed to lucrative contracts. Curtis went 10-8 and Wise 6-8. In their final year with the Padres, Randy Jones was 5-13, and Rollie Fingers saved 23 games with a 11-9 record.

Although fun is poked at Jerry's one-season managerial career, he did guide the Padres to a 73-89 record, which at the time was the team's second-best record ever.

Chapter 4

The Good, the Bad, and the Ugly

Take No Series for Granted

The major accomplishment of the 1969 Padres during the inaugural year occurred in the final month of the season. The mighty Los Angeles Dodgers, in the midst of a five-team battle for the Western Division pennant, came to Mission Valley for a four-game series that included a weekend in sunny San Diego. Many of the Dodgers players and executives brought their families for what was expected to be vacation time. After all, the Dodgers had manhandled the expansion Padres in nine-of-11 games, which included lopsided scores of 19-0, 14-0, 11-0, 10-1 and 9-1.

San Diego chose outfielder Al "The Bull" Ferrara from the Dodgers in the expansion draft. He was to have an outstanding series against the Blue. "You might say I get up for them more than I do the Montreal Expos. I've got no bad feelings toward any of the players over there. I hope they win it, but some of their front office people have made some smart remarks in the past. Some said I couldn't play anymore."

Ferrara certainly proved he could still play. His double and home run accounted for all the runs in a 3-0 San Diego victory in the first game. Gary Ross, who also had special motivation, pitched six shutout innings. Earlier in the season, another Dodgers official crowed, "If we can't beat somebody named Gary Ross, then we don't deserve to be in the pennant race."

The next night, Joe Niekro recorded a 4-1 complete-game victory as Nate Colbert homered and Ferrara made a run-saving catch in the seventh inning.

"What's gotten into that team?" asked perplexed Dodgers coach Jim Gilliam.

The situation only got worse for the Dodgers on Saturday. Padre pitchers Clay Kirby, Tommie Sisk, and Billy McCool would have a combined 8-33 record in 1969, but on this night, they combined to beat the Dodgers 3-1. Ferrara contributed an RBI double.

Al Santorini completed the four-game sweep on Sunday afternoon, pitching the Padres to a 4-2 triumph. Down 2-1 in the seventh, the Padres rallied for three runs to pull it out.

"You donkeys, you don't have any right to beat us," screamed Dodgers outfielder Len Gabrielson.

After he calmed down, Gabrielson allowed, "They're in last place, but they're hustling like crazy, and their young pitchers are starting to mature."

The four-game Padres sweep was the first time in over three months that the club had won more than two straight. The Dodgers began the series in a virtual tie for first place and ended the series two and a half games behind San Francisco. Los Angeles never recovered, and the Atlanta Braves eventually won the West in 1969.

First No-Hitter in San Diego

The first official no-hitter at San Diego Stadium took place June 12, 1970. It was the early game of a twi-night doubleheader between the Padres and the Pittsburgh Pirates. Dock Ellis accomplished the feat in a most unusual fashion. Ellis was wild, walking eight batters and hitting another. The Padres were able to steal three bases. Ellis pitched only three "one-two-three" innings, but the game was over in two hours, 13 minutes. The Bucs' only runs came on a pair of solo homers by Willie Stargell. Ellis later admitted he was "high" on drugs and actually remembered very little about the game. Dave Campbell and Chris Cannizzaro were two Padres in the lineup that day.

Campbell was impressed with the performance. "Ellis had a fast ball that sailed. I always thought when he was at his best, his stuff was as good as any pitcher in the league."

"The game was played in the twilight," Cannizzaro recalled, "which made it tough to see, and Ellis changed speeds well with a natural cutter."

Ellis now makes appearances warning youths about the dangers of drug usage. Incidentally, the Padres won the nightcap of the doubleheader 5-2.

A Loooong Night

The longest night of baseball in San Diego took place September 24, 1971, between the Padres and Houston Astros—another twinight doubleheader. The first game went 21 innings and lasted five hours, 25 minutes before the Padres lost 2-1, when a balk was called on San Diego reliever Gary Ross. Ken Forsch was the starting pitcher for Houston and went 13 innings. Clay Kirby, the Padres starting pitcher, worked 15 innings, giving up eight hits and striking out 15. Kirby threw 232 pitches. Bob Barton caught all 21 innings in the game, but 34 years later confessed, "I don't remember if I thought Ross had balked or not. I guess I was too tired."

He wasn't too tired to catch several more innings of the second game, though.

The second game was tied 4-4 in the ninth inning when the game had to be halted because of dense fog in the San Diego River valley. After a 14-minute delay, the game was resumed at 2:30 a.m. Astros rightfielder Jim Wynn immediately lost Ollie Brown's fly ball in the pea soup, and the winning run scored for San Diego. It was officially seven hours, 39 minutes of baseball before a hardy crowd of 6,339.

Another Loooong Night

The Padres' longest road game also lasted 21 innings (five hours, 33 minutes), and was played on May 21, 1977, at Olympic Stadium in Montreal. The Padres finally won the game 11-8 on a three-run homer in the 21st inning by Merv Rettenmund, who later became the Padres' batting coach. The Expos outhit San Diego 25 to 13 and left 23 runners on base as they suffered their 11th straight defeat. The Padres did not return to their Montreal Hotel until after 2 a.m.

The next day, Rettenmund and Doug Rader decided to psyche out the Expos before the get-away afternoon game. The two players arrived early and made certain the Montreal players saw them playing catch and running around the field. Alas, all it did was tire them out, and the Expos snapped their 11-game losing streak with a 3-1 win.

Yet Another Loooong Night

Easily the longest night of Padre baseball was July 2, 1993. The Padres and Phillies played a doubleheader in Philadelphia with the first game set to begin at 4:35 p.m. Rain delayed the start until 5:45—but was just the beginning. During the game, there were two more rain delays, totaling four hours and 44 minutes. The first contest finally concluded at 1:03 in the morning with the Padres winning 5-2.

Jerry Coleman, Ted Leitner, and I were sharing broadcast duties that night, with Coleman scheduled to fly out early Sunday morning for a CBS Radio broadcast. Ted and I sent Jerry back to the hotel to get some sleep while we began the second game, which started at 1:28 a.m. During the "nightcap," there were several calls to our broadcast booth from talk shows around the country that couldn't believe we were still playing baseball.

The Padres were leading 5-1 in the fifth inning when Ricky Jordan hit a three-run homer off Andy Benes, who later said his slider didn't break too well at 3 a.m. Philadelphia finally won the game 6-5 in 10 innings with the winning run crossing the plate at 4:40 a.m.

It was after 5:30 a.m. when Ted and I returned to the hotel. As we prepared to enter the elevator, Jerry walked out to catch his flight for the CBS broadcast.

What a night. . . .

Missed By That Much

On September 2, 1972, the Padres came within one pitch of having a perfect game thrown against them. The drama unfolded at Chicago's Wrigley Field, with Milt Pappas pitching for the Cubs. Pappas had retired 26 straight batters before facing pinch-hitter Larry Stahl. The count went full before home plate umpire Bruce Froemming ruled that the next pitch was barely outside. Stahl walked to end the perfect game. Pappas retired the next hitter, Garry Jestadt, to complete his no-hitter. He was furious over a call he felt ruined his bid for immortality. On the other hand, Stahl never felt he got enough credit for spoiling the perfect game. Legend has it that several Chicago sportswriters knocked on the umpires' dressing room door after the game. When Froemming appeared, one of the writers commented, "Bruce, you could have been famous as the 12th umpire in baseball history to call a perfect game."

"Oh, yeah?" Bruce replied. "Name the other 11!"

Pefect for Nine Innings

Pedro Martinez of the Montreal Expos pitched nine perfect innings against the Padres on June 3, 1995, but did not receive credit for a no-hitter or a shutout. The Padres' Joey Hamilton was also on his game. After nine innings, neither team had scored. Hamilton had allowed only three hits. In the tenth, the Expos scored a run off reliever Brian Williams to take a 1-0 lead. In the bottom of the inning, Bip Roberts ended the no-hitter with a double to right field. Mel Rojas came in to relieve Pedro. His wild pitch moved Roberts to third. Steve Finley, Tony Gwynn, and Ken Caminiti all failed to get the run home, and the Expos had a 1-0 win. Martinez struck out nine in his nine-plus innings of work in what has to have been the best nine innings of pitching in San Diego history.

I asked Gwynn what made Martinez so tough?

"That night his stuff was electric. He was throwing fastballs at 97 and his change-up at 76 with the same arm motion for both pitches. He also had a good overhand curve, and his control was excellent. It was one of those games where you were just not going to hit him."

Norman Conquers the Big Red Machine

Southpaw Fred Norman threw one of the Padres' best games ever on September 15, 1972, against the Big Red Machine in Cincinnati. Cito Gaston's homer was the only run of the game as Norman struck out 15 Reds in his memorable performance. Freddie fanned every man in the Cincinnati lineup at least once, preserving victory by striking out Bobby Tolan with runners on first and third to end the game.

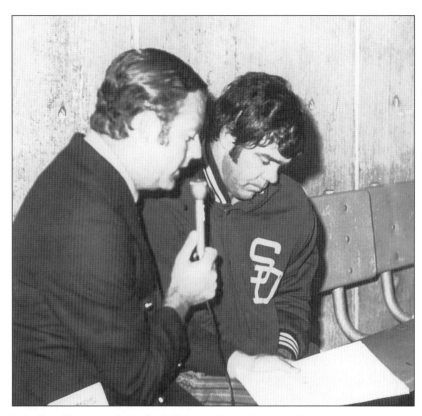

Bob Chandler interviews fred Norman in the Padres dugout.
from the Bob Chandler collection

"That's the worst I've ever seen a group of hitters look," commented Reds manager Sparky Anderson.

Eleven different Reds whiffed against Norman. Johnny Bench, Tony Perez, Dennis Menke, and Don Gullett all went down twice. Also striking out were Pete Rose, Joe Morgan, Bobby Tolan, Dave Concepcion, Cesar Geronimo, Julian Javier and Hal McRae. The Reds were so impressed, they traded for Norman in June 1973.

Of course, the Padres also got some cash in the deal.

No Need to Shower

On August 23, 2005, the Padres' Jake Peavy and the Houston Astros' Roger Clemens hooked up in a terrific pitchers duel with

Peavy and the Padres coming out on top 2-0 in a game that lasted one hour, 53 minutes. A young TV producer asked me if that was the fastest game in Padres history.

The answer is no—not even close.

On May 4, 1977, veteran lefthander Jim Kaat of the Phillies was using a hurry-up style to deliver the ball to the plate, and Padres lefthander Randy Jones always threw low-walk, low-pitch games. The pair battled at San Diego Stadium on a Wednesday night, with Jones winning a 4-1 decision in one hour, 29 minutes—the fastest game in San Diego history.

Kaat told me that he was a Kenny Rankin fan. "Kenny was performing that night at the open-air theater at San Diego State. I had tickets but figured I would arrive after the show began. Our game at the stadium started at 7:05, and the Rankin concert began at 9:00. I was actually sitting in my seat when the music started."

"It's a Good Thing I Don't Have a Fourth Pitch."

The opening home game of the 1987 Padres season produced a most unusual start by the Giants' Roger Mason. The first three hitters in the San Diego lineup all homered. It was the first time in major league history that a team began a season with three consecutive home runs. Mason explained that Marvell Wynne hit a slider, Tony Gwynn connected with a fastball, and John Kruk blistered a split-fingered fastball.

"I tried everything," said Mason, "It's a good thing I don't have a fourth pitch!"

The Giants came back to hit five home runs and win the game 13-6 in Larry Bowa's debut as the Padres manager. Predictably, the fiery Bowa wasn't around at the finish because umpire Bob Engel tossed him for arguing a call in the eighth inning. When you add the normal opening-day festivities and fireworks, it was anything but a boring start to the new season.

Crazy Way to End the Season

The already tumultuous 1973 season ended in bizarre fashion. During the summer, the Padres were rained out in Pittsburgh. It was decided the game would not be made up unless it had a bearing on the pennant race.

On Saturday, September 29, the Padres played what they thought would be their final game ever at San Diego Stadium. The season concluded on a Saturday because the Chargers had the stadium on Sunday.

Several of the Sunday baseball games had to turn out a certain way to require a makeup game in Pittsburgh on Monday. I was attending the Chargers game, and midway through the third quarter, the baseball results indicated we would be flying to the Steel City. The players were all aware of the situation. We met at the airport for a 4:00 p.m. charter flight.

Pittsburgh trailed the New York Mets by one and a half games. While the Pirates hosted the Padres, the Mets were scheduled to play a doubleheader at Chicago. A tie for the division title was possible.

Amazingly, only 2,572 fans showed up at Three Rivers Stadium for the game. Randy Jones took the mound for San Diego. In the fifth inning, Pirates pitcher Dave Giusti looked up in the press box at Pittsburgh announcer Bob Prince, who gave him the thumbs-down sign. The Mets had won the first game in Chicago, and the Bucs were eliminated.

"The Pirates were easy after that," Jones said.

The Padres won 4-3, and Randy finished the season 7-6 for a Washington-bound team that wound up 60-102.

The Padres returned to San Diego not knowing what the future held. Less than four months later, a man named Ray Kroc entered the picture. The rest is history.

Never Give Up

Pittsburgh was also the opponent for the greatest single-game comeback in Padres history. The Pirates were leading San Diego 8-0 in the eighth inning on June 10, 1974. The Padres scored four runs in the bottom of the inning and added five in the ninth to snatch an incredible 9-8 victory.

Pittsburgh starter Jim Rooker was cruising into the eighth with a five-hit shutout when Pirates manager Danny Murtaugh decided to give his bullpen some work. Then Cito Gaston's three-run homer capped a four-run rally for the Padres, but it was still 8-4 Pittsburgh entering the last stanza. Dave Winfield homered with one out to make it 8-5. The Padres loaded the bases. Two were out when Derrel Thomas singled a run home to make it 8-6.

San Diego had already used its entire bench when bullpen catcher Bob Barton was called in to pinch-hit.

"For one of the few times in my life, I was actually dozing in the pen when coach Whitey Wietelman awakened me with a poke in the side," remembered Barton. "I thought they wanted me to warm up a pitcher, but Whitey said, 'No, they want you to pinch hit.' I didn't have my regular cleats on and had to send a bat boy to get them from my locker as everybody waited for me to hit."

Submariner Kent Tekulve was on the mound. Tekulve eventually developed into one of the top relievers in baseball, but in 1974 he was a raw rookie.

"I had never seen him before, and I must have missed his first two pitches by a foot," said Barton. "With the count 0-2, I moved up on the plate and lined a single to left to tie the game 8-8."

Horace Clarke was the next hitter and drilled a 0-2 pitch to center field to win the game for the Padres 9-8.

A footnote to the game was Jim Rooker. He had showered and already left the dressing room by the time the media entered. However, a young sidebar reporter interviewed somebody standing in front of Rooker's locker. Masquerading as Rooker, the individual ripped Danny Murtaugh for taking him out of the game. The story received big play in the paper the next morning.

Rooker was summoned to Murtaugh's office quickly to explain his comments. Jim knew nothing about what was said. The misunderstanding was quickly resolved, but added another element to the Padres' amazing comeback.

A Day to Remember

Fred Kendall was the Padres' primary catcher from 1973-76. On June 24, 1974, Fred's wife, Patty, gave birth to a son, Jason Daniel Kendall, who eventually would become an all-star catcher in the National League.

It was quite a day for Fred. "I took Patty to the hospital about one o'clock in the morning, and she gave birth at 7:25. I got to bed around nine and slept until one in the afternoon, when I left for the ballpark." When Kendall walked into the Padres locker room, he saw his name in the starting lineup. He was batting seventh.

Kendall proceeded to belt a three-run triple in the sixth inning and catch a six-hit shutout pitched by Bill Greif. It was a day that Fred (and Patty . . . and Jason) will never forget. It was also one of the easiest postgame interviews I ever did.

Finally One Million

Playing in a beautiful downtown ballpark, the Padres hope to make drawing three-million fans a season a common occurrence. What a difference 30 years can make! On September 18, 1974, the Padres went over the one-million mark in home attendance, and the city was euphoric. The club staged a one-million-fan promotion, giving away five new cars and 20 television sets. All 33,237 fans in attendance received a bumper sticker that read: "One million Padre fans. I was there."

When the million-mark milestone was announced over the P.A. system, the crowd treated itself to a 20-second standing ovation.

Padres president Buzzie Bavasi received a note from Mayor Pete Wilson. "He said it looked like we were vindicated for believing all along San Diego was a good baseball town."

Why all the excitement? In five years of play in the National League, the Padres' best previous attendance was 644,272 in 1972. The 1974 figure reached 1,075,399. They eclipsed one million again in 1975. The first time the Padres reached the two-million mark was 1985, when 2,210,352 watched the defending National League champs in action. 2004 was the first season in Petco Park, and 3,016,752 paid to watch the Padres. In 1974, the idea of drawing three million fans would have seemed impossible.

What's That Sign Again?

Baseball games are won in many different ways, and some of them are strange. On April 15, 1975, the Padres were playing the Giants in San Francisco. The Giants were leading 1-0 in the eighth

inning when the Padres' leadoff hitter reached first base. Manager John McNamara sent a fleet-footed backup outfielder named John Scott into the game as a pinch runner. On the first pitch, Scott stole second. To the amazement of third-base coach Joey Amalfitano, Scott stole third on the second pitch. The Padres quickly tied the score and went on to beat the unnerved Giants 2-1.

After the game, McNamara revealed he had twice given the bunt sign and twice Scott thought it was the steal sign. Asked if he would fine Scott for his mistakes, McNamara smiled and said, "Of course, but it will be a very small fine."

The two stolen bases were the only bases Scott swiped that year. He was sent to the minors after only nine at-bats.

Who Did You Say Had The Longest Hitting Streak?

Tony Gwynn retired with over 3,000 base hits and a lifetime batting average of .338. However, his longest batting streak in 20 seasons of major league play was 25 games, which is not even close to the Padres' record.

Catcher Benito Santiago holds the San Diego record, hitting safely in 34 consecutive games during his rookie season of 1987. Santiago began the streak on August 25 with a three-run homer in a 5-1 win over Montreal. The streak ended in the next-to-last game of the season, on October 3 against the Dodgers' Orel Hershiser. It was a game the Padres won 1-0 to snap a nine-game losing streak. Even though Santiago was second in the batting order to maximize his plate appearances, he only got three at-bats . . . a strikeout, a groundout, and a fly out.

In 21 of the 34 games, Benito had just one hit. He achieved that hit in his final at-bat five times, including a bunt single in the eighth inning of the October 1 game against Cincinnati.

Benito was batting .284 when the streak began and finished the season at an even .300. It was the longest hitting streak ever for a rookie and for a Latin player. Unsurprisingly, Santiago was the unanimous choice for National League Rookie of the Year.

Chapter 5

Early Padres Stars

Nate, Don't Let Your Head Get Too Big

Nate Colbert hit his first home run for the Padres in 1969. His 163 career homers wearing the brown and tan remain the best in team history. Colbert was the Padres' first slugging star, but he was not their starting first baseman on opening day of that first season in Mission Valley. That honor belonged to six-foot-seven Bill Davis, who batted fifth in the lineup. Much was expected of Davis, but unfortunately, he only hit .175, with one RBI, no home runs, and disappeared.

On April 24, Nate Colbert got his chance at first base. In Houston, he belted a 430-foot, three-run homer in the eighth inning to give the Padres a 4-1 win—the first of 24 home runs he would hit that initial season. Nate would go on to blast 38 home runs in both 1970 and 1972. (It is important to note that there was an 18-foot-high outfield wall at San Diego Stadium until 1982 when shorter portable fences were installed.)

On July 20, 1969, the Padres were playing the Braves in Atlanta. Thanks to a Nate Colbert home run, they carried a lead into the seventh inning. Nate was approaching the batter's box when the Atlanta crowd stood and cheered. Colbert had tears in his eyes as he went back to the on-deck circle where his roommate Cito Gaston waited his turn.

"Roomie," Colbert said, "I can't believe these fans cheering for an opposing player like this."

"Nate, don't let your head get too big," Gaston responded. "Look at the scoreboard."

The scoreboard reported that man had landed on the moon for the first time.

• • •

The 1972 Padres struggled to score runs, denting the plate just 488 times the entire season. Colbert drove in 111 of those runs, accounting for 23 percent of the team total—then a major league record. Nate's 38 home runs in 1972 gave him a four-year total of 127. In 1972, only two active major leaguers had hit more home runs after four seasons: Willie Mays (148) and Frank Robinson (134).

Five Homers with 13 RBIs in a Doubleheader

On August 1, 1972, Nate Colbert put on one of the greatest power displays in major league history. He belted five homers with 13 RBIs in a doubleheader sweep of the Braves in Atlanta's Fulton County Stadium. Ironically, Colbert almost didn't play that day. He had a persistent back problem and approached manager Don Zimmer.

"Zim, my back is killing me. I don't think I can make it today."

Zimmer told him to take a few swings in batting practice and see how it felt.

"I took 10 swings and hit all 10 out of the park," Nate said.

This prompted Zimmer to say, "You can't sit out these games."

Colbert relented, "I'm in there."

In his first at bat, Nate hit a three-run homer and added another home run in the seventh as the Padres cruised to a 9-0 win.

Zimmer was pleased. "Good game, Big Man."

"I'm not through yet, Zim," Nate responded. Truer words were never spoken.

In the second game, Colbert connected for a grand-slam homer in the second inning. In the seventh, he whacked a two-run homer. In the ninth, the big first baseman came up against submariner Cecil Upshaw, a pitcher who always caused problems for him. Nate was having such a hot day that Upshaw decided to fool him by coming

Padres coach Bob Skinner (left) holds five baseballs to represent the five home runs hit by Nate Colbert (right) during a doubleheader in Atlanta on August 1, 1972. The big first baseman also drove in 13 runs that day.
From the Whitey Wietelmann collection

overhand. Colbert crushed his fifth—and longest—home run of the day to deep left-center as the Padres won 11-7.

As he was rounding second, Nate told his friend, umpire Bruce Froemming, "Bruce, I don't believe it."

"I don't either," Froemming joked, "because I've seen you play!"

Nate laughed all the way home. He received his biggest thrill of the day when he took his position at first base. Hank Aaron stopped and told him, "That's the greatest thing I've ever seen."

Colbert's five home runs in a doubleheader tied the major league record set by Stan Musial in 1954. His 13 RBIs in a twin bill established a new major league mark. To add to the irony of the situation, Colbert, as an eight-year-old youngster, was at Sportsman's Park in St. Louis when Musial hit those five homers on May 2, 1954.

Easy Math Would Give Colbert 55 Home Runs

Twice in his Padre career, Nate Colbert hit 38 home runs. According to Nate, he also hit 17 fly balls that bounced off the outfield wall in 1972. Easy math would give Colbert 55 home runs had the inner fence been installed at that time. One could assume that some fly balls were caught against the wall, which also would have cleared the inner fence. Although pure speculation, it's fun to suggest Nate might have broken Roger Maris's record of 61 homers had the inner fence been in place during the 1972 season.

The Best Athlete

Nate Colbert may have been the greatest slugger in Padres history, but easily the best athlete was Dave Winfield. Winfield was a six-foot-six, 225-pound all-around athlete who played varsity basketball and baseball at the University of Minnesota. He was the best pitcher and the best hitter on the Gophers' baseball team, and the Padres made him their number-one draft choice in June 1973.

Winfield's final collegiate game was for the championship in the College World Series. Dave started against USC and led 7-0 with 15 strikeouts heading into the last inning. Winfield was removed after giving up two runs. He went to the outfield, where he watched Southern California stage an incredible rally and win the game 8-7. Minnesota's coach wanted Winfield to come back and pitch, but his arm was hanging, having already thrown 145 pitches. Another factor was the 1-0 shutout victory that he had pitched just two days earlier.

Without a doubt, there's some Babe Ruth in Dave Winfield.

"Big Boy, We Want You To Swing That Bat!"

Padres scout Don Williams signed Winfield. Naturally, Dave wanted to know if the Padres wanted him to pitch or play in the outfield.

"Big boy, we want you to swing that bat four times every day," Williams said.

The first time Winfield had a chance to swing that bat for the Padres was June 19, 1973. The big man was awed by the stadium's

The best athlete to ever play for the Padres was big Dave Winfield.
From the San Diego Hall of Champions Collection

size. Even though he was a basketball star, the outfield wall looked very high. Winfield started in left field and went one for four against Houston, who won 7-3, handing the Padres their 10th straight loss and dropping their record to 20-46. The 1973 Padres were a terrible team that would lose 102 games, so they could afford to promote a player straight from college to the major leagues.

Winfield's first hit was a sharp grounder off the glove of Astros third baseman Doug Rader. Dave beat the throw to first with a head-first slide.

"I didn't really know yet what it took to be successful at the major league level," Winfield said. "So I went all out for the hit and was thrilled when the umpire gave the safe sign."

The Worst Collision

Winfield held his own in 1973, batting .277 in 56 games with three home runs. However, the Padres were loaded with outfielders when spring training began in 1974, and Winfield was ticketed for Triple-A.

Willie McCovey had been obtained from San Francisco, which moved Nate Colbert to left field. Bobby Tolan, John Grubb, Cito Gaston, and Matty Alou were the other outfielders on the roster. Seemingly, there was no room for Winfield in the outfield, but the big guy kept hitting, which made it a tough decision for manager John McNamara. In one spring training game, Mac even played Winfield at shortstop.

"I was as nervous as you could be . . . I hadn't played the position in years [since high school]," remembered Winfield. Dave actually did well at shortstop but never played the position again. The hits continued, though, including one that clinched a game late in the spring training season.

McNamara decided he had to keep Winfield and find a way to get him into the lineup. Dave admits that I was the first to tell him that he'd made the team—during a postgame interview in which I was congratulating him for his game-winning hit. Winfield played 145 games that year and led the team with 75 RBIs to go with 20 homers and a .265 batting average. He would finish his career without ever playing in the minor leagues.

In mid-season, the Padres started an outfield of Colbert in left, Winfield in center, and Gaston in right—a thunderous herd that was perhaps the largest outfield in Padre history. Colbert was six foot two, 220 pounds; Winfield was six foot six, 225; and Gaston was six foot three, 210. During the game, a drive was hit to left-center field with Colbert and Winfield both in hot pursuit.

"I'm running hard, going all out, when I backhanded the ball completely stretched out," Winfield recalled.

The ground seemed to shake as Winfield and Colbert collided at full speed.

"I didn't lose consciousness," explained Winfield. "I just lay there wondering what was broken. Fortunately, neither of us was hurt, and we didn't miss any games. It still ranks as the worst collision I ever experienced in major league baseball."

"The Biggest, Loudest, Longest Ovation of My Career"

Winfield represented the Padres at the 1977, 1978, and 1979 All-Star games—1978 was special because it was the first All-Star game hosted in San Diego.

"At the time, it was the most wonderful thing to happen to me," reminisces Dave. "When I was introduced, I received the biggest, loudest, longest ovation of my career."

In 1979, Winfield received over three million votes, becoming the first Padres player voted to start the All-Star game. Only Phillies Hall of Fame third baseman Mike Schmidt received more votes than Winfield did that year—Dave's finest season as a Padre. He batted .308 with 34 homers and a career-high 118 RBIs, which led the National League. Although playing for a team that finished fifth in the NL West with a 68-93 record, Winfield finished third in the vote for league MVP.

"The Man Who Hit 118 Home Runs Last Year"

Like many great athletes, Winfield had an ego. In 1979, he complained about his supporting cast on the Padres. I remember a time during spring training in 1980, when Dave walked into the Yuma, Arizona, clubhouse.

"Here comes Dave Winfield!" yelled Ozzie Smith. "The man who hit 118 home runs last year."

"What are you talking about Ozzie?" Winfield responded.

"You must have hit 118 home runs," repeated Smith, "because you said nobody ever got on base in front of you."

Everybody laughed, including Winfield.

Wearing a Padres Cap for Hall of Fame Plaque

In 2001, Dave Winfield was inducted into Baseball's Hall of Fame at Cooperstown wearing a San Diego Padres cap. Dave played for six major league organizations during his career, but it boiled down to entering the Hall as either a Yankee or a Padre.

"The glitter of the Yankees with Babe Ruth, Lou Gehrig, Joe DiMaggio, and others was alluring," Winfield admitted. "But when it came down to it, I selected the team that gave me my first opportunity to play."

Winfield is now a vice president and senior advisor for the Padres and serves on the club's board of directors.

"I Had Already Given Up Home Runs to Mays and Aaron. . . ."

Randy Jones was the Padres' first 20-game winner and the team's first recipient of the Cy Young Award. Some 30 years later, he remains one of the most popular all-time San Diego Padre players. Making numerous public appearances and signing thousands of autographs at his popular Randy Jones Barbecue stands at Petco Park certainly help keep him in the limelight.

Randy was 8-1 at the Padres' Double-A farm team in Alexandria, Louisiana, when he was called up to the majors in June 1973. He made his first appearance in relief against the New York Mets on June 16.

"I was scared to death," remembered Jones. "It was Shea Stadium, in front of a big crowd. The Mets were leading 11-1, and Don Zimmer decided to let me get my feet wet."

Randy set the Mets down in order in the seventh inning, but as he came out for the eighth, young third baseman Dave Roberts asked him, "You know who's up?"

Randy turned around. "I do now—it's Willie Mays!" Randy quickly got ahead of Mays for a 1-2 count.

"And then I decided to throw him a sinker over the plate, and the ball must have traveled 500 feet over the left-field wall. It just disappeared into the darkness he hit it so hard. It was the first big-league hit that I ever allowed." It was one of six home runs Willie hit in 1973—his last year in the major leagues.

Randy's next appearance and first start for the Padres was on June 22, against the Atlanta Braves at San Diego Stadium, which he remembered well. "In the first inning, the Braves got two men aboard, and Hank Aaron came to the plate. He hit my second pitch into the left-center field bleachers. So, in about three innings of pitching, I had already given up home runs to Mays and Aaron. I settled down after Aaron's homer and ended up losing 4-3."

Jones actually ended the 1973 season with a respectable 7-6 record and 3.16 ERA in 19 starts. However, 1974 was another story. Randy became a rare 20-game loser with an 8-22, 4.46 mark in 34 starts.

"I was 7-13 and pitching okay at the All-Star break, but in the second half, I totally lost confidence and was pitching defensively. I was 1-9 the second half, and there was talk of using me in relief in 1975."

It wasn't all Randy's fault in 1974. The Padres were blanked in seven of his losses—and scored just one run in seven others. Former Padres manager Preston Gomez was managing Houston in 1974 and observed, "There isn't a team in baseball that wouldn't like to have Randy Jones."

An Invitation to the All-Star Game

A complete reversal occurred in 1975, when Tom Morgan arrived as the Padres' new pitching coach. "He immediately adjusted my mechanics so I was using my body more in the delivery," remembered Jones. The results were dramatic. In spring training, Jones gave up just two runs and 11 hits in 21 innings, and the Padres made him their opening-day starter.

The frustration of the previous year immediately reared its ugly head. Jones shut out the Giants for nine innings, but ended with a no-decision on opening day. Jim Barr of San Francisco pitched 10 innings of shutout ball, and the Giants prevailed 1-0.

"He pitched too well not to win," noted Randy's catcher, Randy Hundley.

One month later, on May 9, Jones pitched 10 shutout innings, recording a 1-0 win over St. Louis when outfielder John Grubb hit a 10th-inning home run. Randy gave up just one hit.

"It was a ground ball by Luis Melendez that just ticked off my glove for an infield single. I believe that game turned around my season and set the stage for the good things to come. I had been frustrated by the lack of offensive support, and this game gave me a huge mental lift."

On July 3, Jones was pitching a perfect game against Cincinnati when the Reds came to bat in the eighth inning. A throwing error by shortstop Hector Torres and an RBI double by backup catcher Bill Plummer ended the perfect game, no-hitter, and shutout, tying the contest 1-1.

"It was a sinker up a little bit," Plummer recalled. "Jones is a good pitcher, and you have to make him get the ball up to do anything against him."

That was all the Reds managed in a 2-1 San Diego victory that helped the left-hander improve to 11-5 with a 1.77 ERA, earning him an invitation to the All-Star Game in Milwaukee.

"I Tried Like the Devil to Get Your Autograph"

Randy remembered walking into the Pfister Hotel coffee shop in Milwaukee during the All-Star break when he saw Yogi Berra, Sandy Koufax, and Don Drysdale sitting at a table. Berra spotted Jones and invited him to join them.

"I almost refused," said Jones. "Berra is an icon, and Koufax and Drysdale were my pitching heroes growing up in Orange County. We had a great conversation, and finally I felt comfortable enough to tell Drysdale that I had learned a great lesson from him."

Of course, Drysdale wanted to know the impact he had made.

"I tried like the devil to get your autograph when I was a kid, and you would never give it to me. I resolved, at that point, that I would never turn down anybody asking me for an autograph."

Berra and Koufax rolled as Drysdale grabbed a napkin, then a pen, and signed his name.

"Here's your damn autograph," Don growled. "Now leave me alone."

• • •

The Padres southpaw was sitting in the National League bullpen chatting with fellow pitcher Andy Messersmith, figuring he wasn't going to pitch as the NL had built a 6-3 lead over the American League.

The phone rang, and Messersmith answered. "Walter Alston [the NL manager] wants you, Randy. He said warm up that little lefthander that gets everybody out."

Randy pitched the ninth, held the AL scoreless, and recorded the save.

The Padres' First 20-Game Winner

The Padres' first 20-game loser became the Padres' first 20-game winner on September 23, when he beat the Dodgers 6-4. It was not a typical Randy Jones game.

"This was more pressure than going for a no-hitter or pitching in the All-Star Game," said Jones who threw 145 pitches that day and survived five Padre errors in the game. "I've never been this tired after a game."

"We wanted him to win 20 so badly that I think all of us were uptight," commented second baseman Tito Fuentes. In the ninth inning, with the Padres leading 6-4, the Dodgers had the tying runs on base with nobody out. Jones retired Tom Paciorek on a groundout and struck out Jim Wynn, when up stepped Steve Garvey.

"I thought, 'Wouldn't you know it, I have to face Garvey, my nemesis, with runners on base in the ninth inning to get my 20th win.'" Garvey lined out to right field, though, and Randy became the first pitcher since 1963 to win 20 games after losing 20 the year before.

"He made a remarkable comeback this year," said Dodgers manager Walter Alston. "He's a tough little pitcher."

Jones would have called it a season after his 20th victory, except he was neck and neck with Tom Seaver and Andy Messersmith for the ERA title going into the last game of the year. Seaver and Messersmith were both scheduled to pitch. Randy took the mound, and his day began badly. The Giants scored three runs in the first inning on a sacrifice fly and two-run homer. Only two of those runs were earned, though, and that's all Jones would allow through seven innings.

Bullpen coach Whitey Wietelmann, in the days before hand-held adding machines and palm pilots, was busy calculating Randy's ERA after each inning and phoning the dugout. By the seventh inning, the great Padres chili cook had determined that Messersmith's final ERA was 2.29 and Seaver's was 2.38. Whitey again rang manager John McNamara and announced that Randy Jones had won the title with a 2.24 ERA.

McNamara sent Gene Locklear to pinch-hit for Jones in the bottom of the inning as the crowd booed, unaware of the situation.

When the voice of public-address announcer John DeMott informed the stadium that Jones had won the title, the crowd exploded.

"I had chills down my spine," Jones remembered as the crowd gave him a 90-second standing ovation, twice calling him out of the dugout for curtain calls.

His final record in 1975 was 20-12 with a 2.24 ERA. He completed 18 of his 36 starts, throwing 285 innings. He would finish second in the Cy Young balloting to the Mets' Tom Seaver.

One of Jones's wins in 1975 required just 68 pitches—a 5-0 shutout win over the Pittsburgh Pirates. The Buccos had a terrific hitting team, but they were a group of free swingers and could not lay off Randy's great sinker. Bob Skinner was the Pirates batting coach at the time and advised his hitters to force Jones to put his pitches higher in the zone. Skinner summed up Jones this way. "His pitches were too good to take and too tough to hit."

"I actually played a little game with myself," Randy told me. "Whenever I retired the first two batters on two pitches, I tried my best to get the next batter out on the next pitch."

Christy Mathewson's Record

Randy Jones was outstanding in 1975, but he was even better in 1976. He went from May 17 until June 26 without walking a batter—a total of 68 innings—tying the immortal Christy Mathewson for a National League record that had stood for 63 years. Randy told me he wasn't even thinking about the record until his pitching coach, Roger Craig, brought it up. Jones had gone 55 innings without issuing a walk when Craig remarked that he had a chance to break Mathewson's record.

"It put the idea in my head," said Randy, "and I couldn't shake it."

Randy was one out away from surpassing Mathewson when he got ahead of San Francisco catcher Marc Hill, 0-2. The next four pitches badly missed the strike zone.

"I absolutely choked—no doubt about it. Hill said if he had known about the record, he would have swung at one of the pitches, but none of them was close enough to the strike zone. It was a choke job," emphasized Jones, who forgot to mention that he had pitched a complete-game 4-2 victory that day for his 13th win of the season— already four more than any other pitcher in baseball. Besides, what's wrong with having your name next to Christy Mathewson in the record book?

Clever John McNamara even had a contingency plan for an intentional walk if one was necessary. The manager was going to move lefty Randy to third base and use Doug "The Red Rooster" Rader to issue the intentional pass.

"Rader was excited about the possibility—too excited, I thought," recalled Jones. "I told him if he threw a pitch over the plate, and the ball was hit to me, I'd kill him."

Fortunately, this never became an issue.

Randy Wins The Cy Young

Randy reached the All-Star break with a 16-3 record. *Sports Illustrated* featured him on the cover and speculated that he might become the first pitcher since Denny McLain in 1968 to break 30 wins.

"I thought I had a good chance. I was totally in the groove, and felt if I received the same run support in the second half of the season that I did in the first half, I could do it."

He started and pitched three shutout innings in the 1976 All-Star game and was voted the Most Valuable Player in the National League's 7-1 victory. Unfortunately, the Padres bats went into hibernation during the second half of the season. In the home stretch, Randy won just six of his final 17 decisions. San Diego was shut out in three of those losses. Seven of his defeats were by a single run. When their ace was on the mound, the Padres hit an anemic .219.

Regardless, Randy Jones was a solid choice for the National League's Cy Young Award. He finished the year 22-14, completing 25 of his 40 starts and posting a 2.74 ERA. He worked a league-high 315 innings and walked just 50 batters.

"A Rubber Band Unraveling"

His 40th and final start of the year might have altered Randy's career. It was September 28 against Cincinnati, and towards the middle of the game, "I felt something pop in my left arm. It was like a rubber band unraveling. I called manager John McNamara to the mound, told him I was done for the year, and left the game."

The Padres closed the 1976 season with a weekend trip to Los Angeles. Jones asked the Dodgers' renowned orthopedic specialist, Dr. Frank Jobe, to check his arm. Jobe probed a bit, then asked Randy to curl his arm to make a muscle. Jones couldn't do it.

"That's not good," commented Jobe.

Randy was deadpan. "I figured that."

Postseason surgery was performed because the doctors could not determine if the problem was a nerve or a biceps tendon. When they opened his arm, it turned out to be the nerve. They sewed him back up because a nerve will regenerate in time. The nerve did come back, only to snap four more times during his career. Randy pitched some good games but was never again the dominant pitcher of 1975 and 1976.

"I still had the sinker, but I could never again throw that good slider."

We will never know if the nerve problem was a cumulative injury or the result of stress during his final start of the '76 season. We do know that he pitched 217 innings in 1974; 285 innings in 1975; and 315 innings in 1976. In 1976, he started 14 games on four days' rest; 22 games on three days' rest, and four games on two days' rest. We also know that, during the seasons of 1975 and 1976, Randy Jones was as good as any pitcher in baseball.

Bob Chandler interviews 1976 Cy Young winner Randy Jones, who remains famous today for his ballpark barbecue and broadcast banter.
From the Bob Chandler collection

Near No-Hitter—Part I
(Clay "The Kid" Kirby)

The Padres have been competing in the National League since 1969 and still have never had a pitcher throw a no-hitter. Several have come close, but the near misses from the early years are best remembered because there was so little else to cheer then.

On July 21, 1970, Padres right-hander Clay "Kid" Kirby pitched eight innings of no-hit ball against the New York Mets. Unfortunately, he was trailing in the game 1-0. The Mets had scored a first-inning run on two walks, a double steal, and a ground out. In the bottom of the eighth, with two outs and nobody on, Kirby was the third scheduled hitter, but Padres manager Preston Gomez sent Cito Gaston in to pinch-hit. Loud boos were heard from the San Diego Stadium crowd of 10,373. Several fans tried to get at Gomez in the Padres dugout.

Bob Skinner was the hitting coach at the time and remembers intercepting a fan. "We didn't think anything about Preston's decision. He was just doing his best to win the game."

The boos got louder when Gaston struck out, and relief pitcher Jack Baldschun immediately gave up a hit and two more runs as the Mets prevailed 3-0.

Gomez said he owed it to the Pittsburgh Pirates to do everything he could to beat the Mets. Even though the Padres were out of the race, Pittsburgh and New York were battling for the Eastern Division title. Gomez told Kirby winning the game is more important than any individual honor, and if he were faced with the same situation, he would do it again.

Kirby was traded to Cincinnati before the 1974 season, and by that time, Preston Gomez was managing the Houston Astros. In a September 4 game between the Reds and Astros, the Kid watched Houston's Don Wilson pitch a no-hitter through eight innings, but the Reds were leading 2-1. When it was Wilson's turn to bat, Gomez sent in Tommy Helms to pinch-hit.

As Yogi Berra would say, "It was deja vu all over again."

After the game, Kirby walked into Preston's office and shook his hand.

Near No-Hitter—Part II (Clay "The Kid" Kirby)

Kirby was only 20 years old when he broke in with the 1969 Padres. Considering his outstanding fast ball and slider, many baseball people felt it was just a matter of time before he pitched a no-hitter. On September 18, 1971, he came close again at Candlestick Park against the Giants. Kirby had a perfect game through seven innings, when he hung a slider for Willie McCovey. Big Mac's home run was the only hit the Giants managed against Kirby in the 2-1 San Diego victory.

Bob Barton was Kirby's catcher that game. "To this day, I second-guess myself for not calling a changeup. McCovey was perfectly set up for the pitch, but I didn't want Clay to lose a no-hitter on his third best pitch."

Clay "the Kid" Kirby was an early Padres pitcher who almost threw three no-hitters. From the San Diego Hall of Champions Collection

Kirby finished with 10 strikeouts and one walk (which immediately followed McCovey's home run). "I thought if I could get McCovey out, I would pitch a perfect game."

Although Kirby never did pitch a no-hitter for the Padres, he came close on a third occasion. In a five-day span during September 1971, the Kid twice took no-hitters into the ninth inning. He lost 3-2 in Houston on September 13, and won the aforementioned one-hitter on September 18. Kirby hurt his arm in the mid-1970s and was out of baseball before his 30th birthday. On October 11, 1991, Clay Kirby died suddenly of a heart attack at the age of 43 in his hometown of Arlington, Virginia.

Near No-Hitter—Part III (Dr. Steve Arlin)

There have been many close calls on no-hitters, but none was closer than when right-hander Steve Arlin came within one strike of the team's first no-no on July 18, 1972.

The Phillies were batting in the ninth with two outs and nobody on base. Slap hitter Denny Doyle was at the plate. Padres manager Don Zimmer had his rookie third baseman, Dave Roberts, play in to guard against the bunt. Arlin got two strikes on Doyle, and Roberts checked with Zimmer, who told him to stay in. Doyle hit a high chopper that would have been an easy out had Roberts played back. Instead, the ball bounced over Roberts's head, and the no-hitter was lost.

Zimmer admitted his mistake. "I screwed it up. I played what I thought were the percentages."

Afterwards, Zimmer approached Arlin and handed him a razor blade. "Go ahead," the manager said, pointing to his throat. "Just make it quick."

Arlin, who settled for a 5-1 win, said he was so engrossed in pitching to Doyle that he was unaware of where Roberts was playing. The Doctor was in the midst of an incredible month. In his last eight starts—covering 71 innings—Steve had allowed just 33 hits.

Incidentally, an audience of 4,764 witnessed the game at San Diego Stadium—it just doesn't sound right to say "a crowd of 4,764."

Chapter 6

Broadcasting

And There It Goes . . .

Before the Major League Padres got their start in 1969, San Diegans cheered the Pacific Coast League Padres, a Triple-A team that existed from 1936-1968. Beginning in the late 1940s until their final season in 1968, radio fans had the pleasure of listening to Al Schuss broadcast Padres games. Schuss was a former FBI agent from Chicago who moved to San Diego because of his wife's health. He was a major league caliber announcer with a rich, deep voice and a signature home run call: ". . . And there it goes."

He had many different partners over the years. For most of the 1960s, his sidekick was Al Couppee, the sports director of KOGO Radio & TV (Channel 10). I was Couppee's assistant from 1963 until 1968 and had an opportunity to watch (and occasionally participate) as these old pros re-created baseball games from Western Union tickertape from far-off places like Indianapolis, Little Rock, and Honolulu. Geographically, the Pacific Coast League had no boundaries after the Dodgers and Giants moved to California in 1958.

Broadcasting baseball live from the ballpark is terrific fun. Re-creating games in the radio studio for most announcers was not nearly as much fun—except for Al Schuss. He loved to do re-creations, and in my view, was outstanding at this unique art form. Many Sunday afternoons, I would be preparing for my evening TV sportscast when Schuss would arrive at the studio to re-create a doubleheader from somewhere. He would carefully set up a table full of notes, statistics, scorebooks, media guides, and articles he might want to talk about during the game. He also had a round wooden stick that he would whack against a suspended bat to simulate the sound of the bat hitting cowhide. Next to him was a chair with a cushion that sounded like a ball hitting the catcher's mitt when he struck the cushion with his wooden stick.

Always Trust the Ticker

The information about the games came over a Western Union ticker with one copy for Schuss and another copy for the disc jockey/engineer in a nearby booth. The disc jockey had various crowd noises he would play according to the game situation. He also had other sound effects he would add from time to time. The information on the ticker was sparse to say the least, so naturally there had to be embellishment to fill air space. For instance B1OS (ball one outside) would translate to something like, "There's a cut-fastball that just misses the outside corner for ball one . . . you can tell the catcher thought the pitch was a strike . . . you can see him saying something to the plate umpire, but he's not turning his head." When the team played in Hawaii, wire service was not available, so the Padres paid one of the sportswriters covering the game to telephone information every few innings. There were times when the announcers would complete their play-by-play before the next phone call was received. That is when serious ad-libbing with plenty of foul balls and an occasional brief rain delay would occur. The games sounded so realistic on radio that many fans thought the broadcasters were reporting live.

Fireman, Where Are You?

When I was sports director of Channel-39 in 1968, then known as KCST-TV, we televised some PCL-Padre games from Phoenix and Denver. Our first games were from Phoenix Municipal Stadium in May. The games were telecast in black and white. Only three cameras were used, and I was the only announcer. This was well before TV producers discovered the centerfield camera, which is the staple shot in a baseball telecast today. Our cameras were located behind home plate, first base, and third base. It was literally about 100 degrees at game time, and 30 minutes before the first pitch, the home-plate camera caught fire. We opened the telecast using only the first-base and third-base cameras, which created a nightmare for the director and probably for the people watching in San Diego as well. By the third inning, the home-plate camera began to work again, which was of considerable help.

The Phoenix Giants were led by a young outfielder named Bobby Bonds. He destroyed the Padres in that series with key hits, including several homers. You can see that some things never change. As far back as 1968, a player named Bonds was hitting home runs to beat San Diego. Immediately following the series, Bobby was called up to San Francisco and proceeded to hit a grand-slam home run that helped beat the Los Angeles Dodgers.

Hill, Here's Your Number

Maybe the most unique hire at Channel 39 was Jim Hill, now a very successful sportscaster for CBS-TV Channel 2 in Los Angeles. In 1968, Channel 39 and the Chargers had an arrangement that the team's number-one draft choice would wear number 39 to help promote the station. We were broadcasting all of their exhibition games, an occasional regular-season game, a weekly highlight show, and Sid Gillman's coach's show. The Chargers actually had two number-one picks in 1968. They chose Russ Washington and Jim Hill.

Washington was a huge tackle who was required to wear a number in the 70s. Hill was a defensive back from Texas A & I, and became number 39. It just so happened that Hill was a radio-TV major in college. The station hired him to help me in sports. He also hosted his own talent show called, *Mr. 39 Talent Time.*

A Creative Goodbye

Jim was a fun guy. After a few years together, the station fell upon hard economic times. Along with many other employees, Jim was without a job. He promised a goodbye that I would never forget. He was right.

My Channel 39 KCST-TV buddies (right to left), Jim Hill, cameraman Les Dodds and me. From the San Diego Hall of Champions Collection

A go-go dancer was one of the staples of his talent show. On his last day at the station, nearing the end of our early 30-minute sportscast, I thought I was going to escape any crazy stunt by Hill.

I was wrong.

I stood behind a wide podium for the sportscast. With one minute to go, I noticed the studio backdrop curtain open at the corner. It was Mr. 39 and his go-go dancer.

With 45 seconds left, I observed the dancer crawl on all fours behind the podium.

With 30 seconds left, I felt a hand on my leg.

With 15 seconds, the hand was moving up my leg.

Finally, "AND THAT'S THE SPORTS. . . ." concluded my sportscast.

Hill (and the go-go dancer) got me good.

I phoned my old boss Al Couppee at Channel 10 and recommended that he find a job for my fun-loving colleague. Couppee hired him, and after a successful stay in San Diego, Jim moved on to bigger and better things in Los Angeles.

The Duke of Flatbush . . . Er, Mission Valley

The first broadcast team for the major league Padres included Jerry Gross, Frank Sims, and Duke Snider. Jerry was a terrific basketball announcer who had come to San Diego from St. Louis to broadcast the newly created NBA San Diego Rockets games. He had also done some work for the baseball Cardinals in St. Louis. Sims had broadcast major league baseball for the Philadelphia Phillies, and later for the Dodgers when they were experimenting with subscription TV in Los Angeles. Snider was a Hall of Fame outfielder for the Dodgers in both Brooklyn and Los Angeles. Gross and Sims were supposed to divide the play-by-play duties with Snider handling color. Duke also helped Padres hitters in spring training and occasionally during the regular season.

Unfortunately, there were problems right from the start. Neither Gross nor Sims officially had been named number one, which created an unhealthy atmosphere as each tried to assume that role. After two years, Sims left the booth to become director of broadcasting and sales. After three years, Gross was not renewed. In the meantime, Duke became the Padres Double-A manager at Alexandria, Louisiana.

Jerry Coleman and I were hired as the broadcast team starting with the 1972 season.

Gross became a successful TV sportscaster at Channel 8. He later broadcast for the Chargers, hosted a sports talk show and did some local hockey play-by-play. He eventually left San Diego but is back again doing some sports radio. Duke's Alexandria Aces won the 1972 Texas League championship. Among the players on that team who would play in the majors were Randy Jones, Dan Spillner, Dave Freisleben, Mike Ivie, John Grubb, John Scott, and Randy Elliott. Snider eventually ended up in Montreal where he broadcast Expos games for 14 years. He is now retired and lives in Fallbrook. Sims matriculated to the Angels, where he served as the team's traveling secretary for several years.

Where's Schuss?

I always felt bad for Al Schuss. The major league Padres tried to separate themselves from anything associated with the minor league team. I understood the theory, but I always felt they missed a bet by not hiring Schuss to do some kind of pre- or postgame show and to occasionally participate in the broadcasts. He did do some games in the late 1970s, but by then his fastball was gone.

In 1970 and 1971, I did the play-by-play on Channel 39 as we telecast 18 games each season (nine from Los Angeles and nine from San Francisco). In those days, there was no satellite to help defray transmission costs, and stations had to use long-distance lines from the telephone company. They were expensive, and the only games that Channel 39 could afford were those from the other California cities.

Duke Snider was my color man during those two seasons. What a thrill. I remember the 1950s when New York boasted three outstanding center fielders who were the toast of baseball: "The Duke" of Brooklyn, the Giants' "Say Hey Kid" Willie Mays, and "The Mick"—Mickey Mantle of the Yankees. The first game I did with Duke at Dodger Stadium was overwhelming for me. I was broadcasting a major league baseball game involving the Padres from historic Dodger Stadium with Duke Snider as my color man. It was a very memorable day, but not the most memorable game I ever did with Duke.

It's Never Over 'Til It's Over

On the afternoon of May 23, 1970, the Padres played a game at Candlestick Park in San Francisco. Giants Hall of Fame pitcher Juan Marichal was on the mound, and San Francisco had staked him to an 8-0 lead after two innings. I could just imagine people in San Diego turning off their television sets. However, the Padres knocked Marichal out of the game with a five-run third inning. They went on to capture an incredible 17-16, 15-inning victory that took five hours,

29 minutes. The Padres used 21 players; the Giants used 22; and each club trotted out seven pitchers. The two teams combined for 44 hits, including nine homers. Willie Mays hit a pair, and Willie McCovey had another for the Giants. Nate Colbert and Cito Gaston were among those who homered for San Diego. The big blow, however, was Steve Huntz's home run in the 15th inning, which proved to be the winning run for the Padres. Duke left the booth in the eighth inning to conduct the postgame interview on the field. He never returned because it appeared that one of the two teams would win as the innings began to string out. In the end, the Padres left 17 runners on base, and the Giants stranded 15.

It was also the final game for Giants manager Clyde King. Charlie Fox was named the new San Francisco skipper the next day. Fox later told me that he was in Portland—in his managerial role for the Phoenix Giants—listening to the game on the radio. The general manager of the Phoenix club, Rosy Ryan, entered. Fox told Rosy that the big-league Giants were having a terrible game. He commented that Clyde King was using up his pitching staff, and there was a doubleheader scheduled for the next day.

"Oh, no. . . . You're in trouble," Rosy said. "You're the new Giants manager tomorrow!"

Buzzie, I Need an Agent

In October of 1971, Buzzie Bavasi hired me as one of the Padres radio-TV announcers. Buzzie was president of the Padres and the former highly respected general manager of the Dodgers in Brooklyn and Los Angeles. I have since told Buzzie that I think he's the reason players decided to hire agents to negotiate their contracts. I was no match for a pro like Buzzie when we did our deal. I remember going into his office with many ideas. After an hour, we stood up and shook hands. In a daze, I asked Buzzie what I'd agreed to do. In addition to broadcasting the games, it was my responsibility to maintain and type out the daily statistics and to run the speakers bureau during the off-season. This was in the early 1970s and there were no computers available. It took me about two hours a day to compute individual player stats from that day's game and then to type them out manually on my portable typewriter. I did learn early that statistics don't lie,

The Padres' first president, Buzzie Bavasi.
From the San Diego Hall of Champions Collection

but liars can use statistics. I could make even the worst Padre teams sound respectable with a judicious application of certain numbers during the broadcast.

Coleman and Chandler

On November 8, 1971, Jerry Coleman and I were named the Padres' new, official broadcast team. I knew Jerry was a member of the great Yankee teams of the 1950s and later was a broadcaster on CBS-TV and for the Bronx Bombers. Jerry actually joined the Yankees full time in 1949 and was the Associated Press Rookie of the Year. In 1950, he was the MVP of the World Series as the Yankees swept the "Whiz Kids" of Philadelphia in four games. In fact, Jerry is one of a dozen players who played on five consecutive World Series Champions from 1949 thru 1953. He retired after the 1957 season. During Jerry's Korean War-interruped nine seasons, the Yankees competed in eight World Series, winning six of them. His broadcasting career in New York included working with such memorable announcers as Dizzy Dean, Red Barber, Mel Allen, Phil Rizzuto, and Joe Garagiola. That is impressive company.

It's been more than 30 years since we began working together, and I still remember the early lessons he taught me. Jerry was patient with his young partner. In 1972, I thought I really knew baseball. It wasn't until several years later that I realized how little I really knew in the beginning.

I've said it before publicly that I learned more about baseball and life from Jerry Coleman than from anybody else in my life.

One important lesson: "Never immediately correct a misstatement made on the air."

For instance, everybody remembers Phillies Hall of Fame third baseman Mike Schmidt. When you're describing rapid play-by-play action on the field, it is easy to mispronounce "Schmidt." It can come out as "Shit." If you say "shit," then immediately say, "I mean Schmidt," everybody knows you messed up.

Jerry would occasionally say something like, "There's a ground ball to Shit . . . he goes to second for one . . . back to first for a double play." The audience is left wondering what was really said, and usually, the broadcaster is given the benefit of the doubt. Once, when Jerry was working a national CBS Radio game with Jack Buck, he made the "Schmidt/Shit" error.

During a commercial break, Buck tried to be polite. "Jerry, you just said shit."

"I know," said Jerry. "Fifth time!"

Wanna Do An Interview?

I estimate that, since 1972, when I began working full time for the Padres, I have conducted roughly 7,000 pre- and postgame interviews on radio and television.

Some good. Some bad. Some strange. Some unusual.

The 1972 Padres had an outfielder named John Jeter, nicknamed "The Jet" because of his speed. Jeter had a mediocre season, batted just .221, and was traded to the Cubs after the season. Still, he had some good games, and I interviewed him multiple times during the year.

During these interviews, Jeter used the term "you know" so often that his teammates in the clubhouse used to keep count. On the last day of the season, we sat together on the bus to the ballpark and chatted for about 30 minutes. At the end of the conversation, Jeter asked me, "By the way, what do you do for the ball club, anyway?"

Obviously, I had made a big impact with my interviews!

Always Keep An Eye Out For Sharon

Like all of the early Padre teams, what the 1975 club lacked in talent, it made up for in characters. Outfielder Dick Sharon hit .194 in what would be his last year in the majors. He loved to pull pranks, and relief pitcher Danny Frisella was one of his co-conspirators. Frisella appeared in 65 games for the 1975 Padres and posted a 3.12 ERA and nine saves to tie Bill Greif for the club lead. During a live postgame interview with Frisella in the Padres dugout, I faced one of my greatest challenges. Sharon arrived on the scene and "de-pantsed" me while I tried to ask questions of Frisella! The audience never knew, but I finished the show with my pants around my ankles. Tragically, Frisella died New Year's Eve, 1975, in a dune buggy accident near Yuma, Arizona.

Where Was That Pitch Again?

Mario Ramirez was Garry Templeton's backup at shortstop for the 1984 Padres. He was used sparingly and batted only .119 for the season. In one game, he hit a double and a home run, so this was a rare opportunity to interview him. It was my impression that Mario just spoke a little English. My interview was intended not to embarrass the likeable Puerto Rican infielder.

"Tell me about the double and home run."

"Bob, the double came off a hanging slider, and the home run was off a fastball, right down the cock."

I guess he'd learned a little more English than I had realized.

Would You Please Repeat That Answer?

Once on our radio pregame show, I asked a shy player a question. He nodded his head in response. Fortunately, it was a taped interview, so I reminded him the listening audience couldn't hear a nod. During a spring training interview, I asked another player what he'd done in the off-season.

He replied, "Oh Bob, that's a tough one."

What Do You Dream About?

Greg Riddoch was a coach for the Padres from 1987 until he took over as team manager midway through the 1990 season. The Padres made a strong run for the Western Division title in 1989 and were optimistic about 1990. I believe the worst seasons are the ones where you expect to win but have a bad year instead. That's what happened in 1990. I asked Riddoch if, in his wildest dreams, he could have imagined the Padres playing so poorly.

Greg answered, "Bob, in my wildest dreams, baseball is the farthest thing from my mind."

Jerry, Let's Change Seats

1974 was the first year of Ray Kroc's ownership. Early in the season, he joined Jerry and me in the broadcast booth and sat between us. Jerry was on the left, and I was on the right. For two innings, Jerry chatted with Kroc, and they had a nice conversation. Then it was my turn. I kept asking Ray questions between calling the play-by-play. The trouble was, except for an occasional, "Eh, what? What did you say?," Ray wasn't answering. I'm sure I broke out in a cold sweat as I struggled through the inning. It wasn't until later that I learned Ray Kroc was almost deaf in his right ear. Nevertheless, I didn't sleep very well that night.

Steve, Can You Clarify That Answer?

Speaking of Coleman, when he managed the Padres in 1980, Steve Mura was one of the pitchers on his staff. Mura was pitching a strong game until he struggled a bit in the eighth inning. Jerry went to the mound for a brief conversation. Mura pitched out of trouble, won the game, and was my guest on the TV postgame show. I asked Mura the words of wisdom that Jerry had imparted when he went to the mound.

Mura's answer was succinct and brutally truthful. "He told me I was pitching horseshit."

How do you clean that up on live television?

The Cough Button

Tommy Jorgensen was our producer/engineer in the radio booth from 1974 until his retirement around 1990. Jorgy was a grizzled radio veteran whom I first met in 1963, when I went to work for the KOGO stations. He was the first to throw out the star at San Diego Stadium when Jerry called for it. Jerry built him into such a personality that, when it was time for the broadcast to begin, announcers at the station would frequently say, "Okay, now let's go out to the stadium broadcast booth with Jorgy and the guys."

Jorgy had built a wonderful device into our microphones called a "cough button." Literally, when one of us needed to cough or relay a message along off the air, we just pressed the button and nobody in Radioland could hear.

One day, while I was calling the action, Jorgy tapped me on the shoulder.

I pressed the cough button and muttered, "What do you want you little SOB?"

He looked me straight in the eyes, and said, "Bob, I just wanted to let you know your cough button is not working tonight." He then watched the color drain from my face as my broadcast career flashed before my eyes.

Fortunately for me, the cough button was working, but a few more gray hairs appeared on my head.

Would You Describe That Play Again?

Some things in baseball just can't be planned. On July 22, 1988, the Padres played the Cubs at Wrigley Field in Chicago. Jerry Coleman and Dave Campbell were broadcasting the game on radio until Campbell became ill and had to leave the booth in the early innings. Jerry was doing the game solo and drank several cups of coffee. It appeared his bladder would hold until the end of the game, but the Padres tied the score 4-4 in the ninth, and the contest was headed to extra innings. In the old Wrigley Field Press Box, there was one restroom and it was located too far away for Jerry to make it back and forth before the next inning began. Finally in the 11th inning, with pressure mounting, the old pro spotted an old waste basket in the corner of the booth. Sometimes drastic measures are necessary, and Jerry thought he had found the solution to his problem. In the bottom of the 11th, the Cubs had Manny Trillo on second base with two out. Lance McCullers was on the mound for San Diego. Cubs catcher Damon Berryhill, who had already doubled and homered, was in the batter's box. Padres manager Jack McKeon ordered an intentional walk, preferring to take his chances with a likely pinch-hitter. A perfect time for the waste basket. After all, what could happen during an intentional walk?

All of sudden, there was a huge roar from the Wrigley faithful, and Trillo was heading home with the winning run. Somehow, the ball was in centerfield. It's tough to call a play like that when you have no idea about what happened. Thinking quick, Jerry Coleman announced that he'd be back with a recap and went to commercial. So what happened? Benito Santiago was in his second season as the Padres regular catcher and possessed a strong throwing arm—he liked to use it, too. Robby Alomar was San Diego's rookie second baseman and was calmly talking to Trillo during the intentional walk. All of

Padres second baseman and broadcaster, Dave Campbell
From the Larry Littlefield Collection

a sudden, Santiago fired a bullet to second, hoping to surprise Trillo and pick him off. He surprised Trillo all right, but he also surprised Alomar. The throw sailed into centerfield. Trillo scored easily, and the game was abruptly over.

Now you know the rest of the story. . . .

A Terrible Day

October 20, 1977, was one of the worst days of my life. I was informed that afternoon that my services were no longer needed by the Padres. I was fired for the first time in my life. I was crushed. Ray Kroc felt Jerry and I should have been talking back and forth more during the broadcast. Actually, I agree with that approach, but Buzzie Bavasi, who came from the Dodgers and the Vin Scully School of broadcasting, had hired us. Even today, when Scully is broadcasting, he has no color commentator. Jerry and I assumed that was the way that management wanted the broadcast. Nobody had told us anything different for six seasons.

Several weeks later, I was hosting a sports talk show on KSDO, and Ray Kroc was my guest. He told me I should have informed him that Bavasi wanted us to broadcast that way. I told Ray it would have been presumptuous for me to go over Buzzie's head to complain. Besides, how did I know that he didn't like what we were doing since we had never been told.

Kroc rehired me several months later as media relations director. By 1979, I was again involved with the broadcast.

Soupy, Want A Job?

In a roundabout way, my dismissal opened the door for Dave Campbell's career as a baseball announcer. Dave had come to the Padres in 1970 from the Detroit Tigers, and over the years, we had become good friends.

The Saturday after I was fired, Dave and I ran into each other following a San Diego State football game. Over a few drinks in the stadium club, Dave told me he had been fired as the manager of the Padres Double-A Amarillo Club in the Texas League. At that point, he didn't know what the future held. My firing had not yet been made public, so I suggested Dave apply for my vacant job. He was good looking, glib, and a former Padres player. I thought he would be a natural for the job. He was reluctant, but applied and eventually was hired to work with Jerry Coleman. He remained a Padre broadcaster through the 1988 season before moving on to ESPN. He is now one of ESPN Radio's top analysts and recently signed a five-year extension.

Pay-Per-View Baseball

In 1984, I moved back into the Padres broadcasting booth on a full-time basis, partly because the Padres and Cox Cable of San Diego had embarked on a joint pay-per-view venture. It was called the San Diego Cable Sports Network and involved 41 home games. Fans could purchase the 41 games for $120, a 20-game package at $70 or individual games for $4.50 each. Cox Cable Executives claimed a market share of approximately 10,000 households per game in 1984 with three to four persons per household. Obviously, Cox and the Padres picked a good season—the Padres won their first pennant that year, and interest was high. Jerry Coleman hosted a pregame show before reporting for his radio duties. Ted Leitner and I shared the play-by-play and color. Ted was also a sportscaster at Channel 8 at the time and occasionally had to leave for the 11:00 p.m. news before the Padres game was over. I often finished announcing the game from our first-base camera position at the far end of the Padres dugout. I was there to interview a player on the postgame show when the game ended. Ted and I worked the cable games until the deal folded in 1993. We also worked together on radio for roughly 20 years. I found Ted a delight as a broadcast partner. He's smart, witty, well-read, and extremely professional. I've said many times that he's the most talented all-around broadcaster I've known while working in the San Diego market since 1961.

The economics of the game drastically affected the Padres in 1993 and 1994. Many of the best players were sold or traded. Fan interest hit rock bottom. Because of this, the Padres and San Diego Cable Sports Network ended their arrangement after 1993. Prime Sports of Los Angeles entered the picture for the next three years and hoped eventually to establish a regional sports network with the Padres as the anchor team in San Diego.

What Do I Do Next?

Perhaps my busiest baseball season ever was 1996. I did a pregame player interview, which was part of a 15-minute prerecorded radio pregame. This was necessitated because I was the main TV play-by-play announcer for Padres games on Prime Sports. After we signed off on television, I went next door to the radio booth and hosted the postgame show with scores and an interview from the field. On the road, I handled the pre- and postgame radio shows live while alternating on radio and television with Coleman and Leitner.

I did not have a regular color man on the Prime Sports Telecasts. Mark Grant and Rick Sutcliffe were both rookie announcers and alternated color on most of the games. Others handling color in 1996 included likeable NBC broadcaster Joe Garagiola, Randy Jones, and Hall of Famer Frank Robinson. Robinson was fun. We did a four-

Bob Chandler interviews Padre-legend Tito Fuentes.
From the San Diego Hall of Champions Collection

game series, and I spent the whole time asking him baseball questions. Much like when he was a player, he never backed away from any subject. Randy Jones and I went back to his rookie season of 1973. We had fun recalling old times as well as commenting on the game at hand. Mark Grant was nervous in the beginning, but with his personality, I had no doubt that he would be a success. Sutcliffe had been an active player through 1995 and was close to many of the players in the league. He obviously knew the game and was able to get terrific inside information. In the beginning, he wasn't sure what to use and what not to use. Occasionally, we had to tone him down. However, he was not intimidated and had the same drive to succeed in the broadcast booth that made him a top pitcher. His subsequent accomplishments are well documented.

Chapter 7

Ray Kroc

What's A Team Worth?

In May of 1973, Padres owner C. Arnholt Smith had reached agreement to sell his team to Washington grocery magnate Joseph Danzansky, who would move the club to the nation's capital in 1974. However, a series of lawsuits placed the Padres in limbo. A judge ruled that San Diego city attorney John Witt could not stop the Padres from going to Washington, but the city did have grounds for damages since 15 years remained on the lease to play at San Diego Stadium. What might a San Diego jury determine the worth of a major league baseball team to a city for a period of 15 years? It was an answer other major league baseball owners did not want to learn. Thus, the 1974 Padres were going to be operated by the National League until an ownership solution could be found. This was the same situation that occurred with the Montreal Expos from 2002 until 2005, when, ironically, they moved to Washington.

"He'll Just Write A Check"

Padres president Buzzie Bavasi's telephone rang, and on the other end was attorney Don Lubin. The lawyer informed Bavasi that he had a potential buyer for the Padres named Ray Kroc. Buzzie did not recognize the name and asked Lubin how this Mr. Kroc proposed to pay for the team.

"Oh, he'll just write a check," Lubin answered.

Buzzie's interest perked up immediately. By the time Bavasi arranged for a lunch meeting between Kroc and C. Arnholt Smith, he learned that Ray Kroc was the founder and chief stock holder of McDonald's Restaurants and one of the richest men in the United States.

"You Want To Buy A Monastery?"

To go back a few months, Ray and Joan Kroc were sailing on their yacht off the Florida Coast when Ray saw an item in the newspaper about the Padres being for sale. He told Joan he was thinking of buying the Padres, and Joan replied, "Why would you want to buy a monastery?" She soon learned the Padres were a major league baseball team located on the California Coast.

Ray Kroc had been a lifelong baseball fan who worked as a salesman in Chicago. Frequently, he would spend an afternoon rooting for his beloved Cubs at Wrigley Field. He once told me he had been in the bleachers in 1938 when Chicago catcher Gabby Hartnett hit the famous "Homer in the Gloamin" to win the pennant for the Cubs. It was late in the afternoon, almost dusk, and if Hartnett had made an out, the game would have been called because of darkness since there were no lights at Wrigley Field. Instead, he homered, and the Cubs played the Yankees in the World Series, where they were swept.

Ray Kroc was 55 years old when he really hit it big with McDonald's. He was selling multi-mixers when he received an order for a large number of mixers from a small restaurant in San Bernardino, California, called McDonald's. Ray could not imagine why a small hamburger joint would need so many multi-mixers for milkshakes, so he traveled to California to observe the restaurant in action. Parked across the street at lunchtime, he watched hundreds of people stop at McDonald's for burgers, shakes, french fries, and quickly return to their work.

The light bulb went on in Ray's brain. What if you had hundreds of these restaurants across the country selling burgers, fries and milkshakes in every city? It took a while, but eventually Kroc made a deal with the McDonald brothers, and his dream became a reality. The first official McDonald's restaurant owned by Kroc still stands in his hometown of Chicago.

"I Should Have Asked For More"

Before his death, C. Arnholt Smith did an interview with Fred Lewis for the *Heart of San Diego* television program. Smith said he and Kroc had a nice lunch with some small talk until Ray asked outright, "I understand you have a baseball team for sale?"

Smith responded, "I don't want to sell the team, but yes, the Padres are for sale."

"How much do you want?" Kroc countered.

"$12 million," Smith answered.

"Deal," said Kroc, who quickly phoned his wife, Joan, to tell her of the transaction. Smith said he had the feeling that if he had said the asking price was $20 million, Kroc still would have purchased the team.

"What Do I Need with More Money?"

The news conference to announce Kroc's purchase of the Padres took place at Smith's Westgate Hotel in late January. Naturally, the room was packed with media. Ray stood alone in front of the large group answering all of their questions. In the Padres' first five years in San Diego, their top seasonal attendance was 644,272 in 1972. Kroc was asked what kind of attendance he expected in 1974. I will never forget his response.

"I don't know, maybe 700,000. . . . After all, what do I need with more money?"

Ray could have hired the best public relations firm in America and not delivered a better reply for the baseball fans of San Diego. In retrospect, why was I surprised? Ray Kroc was arguably the greatest merchandiser in the history of the United States. Incidentally, despite the fact his team would lose 102 games in 1974, attendance soared to over one million. In the early 1970s, that was the benchmark for success in major league baseball.

The San Diego chapter of the Baseball Writers Association of America used to host a preseason Padres banquet as a kick off to the season. In April 1974, the function was held at the Town & Country Convention Center. A huge crowd attended, with most people milling around the foyer during a pre-dinner cocktail party. When Ray Kroc entered the building, people spontaneously clapped as soon as they recognized him. The ovation grew as fans responded to the man they felt had saved major league baseball for San Diego. I looked closely at Kroc, and the gleam in his eye was something I'll never forget. I'm sure Ray had been cheered and applauded at various McDonald's gatherings, but probably never like he was by the fans that night at the Town & Country Hotel.

Ray Kroc Took The Public Address Microphone

Even though legitimate major league names were added to the menu for the first time in team history, the 1974 Padres were not a good team. For starters, when Big Mac became available, naturally the McDonald's owner had to have him. Aging Willie McCovey, arriving from the San Francisco Giants, would be his biggest name and biggest draw. Infielder Glenn Beckert came from the Chicago Cubs, and Bobby Tolan was acquired from Cincinnati. Finally, veteran outfielder Matty Alou was purchased from the St. Louis Cardinals. John McNamara was beginning his first season as the manager. The team looked good on paper.

The club began the season in Los Angeles and got blown out three straight by the Dodgers, a preview of the 102-loss season to come. April 9 was the Padres' first home game for Ray Kroc, and it would prove to be memorable.

Over 39,000 fans showed up for the game and were disappointed as the Houston Astros took a 9-2 lead into the seventh inning. John DeMott was the Padres' public address announcer at the time and remembers Ray Kroc entering his booth just as the Padres had loaded the bases. Ray told John he wanted to address the crowd after the Padres batted. Slugger Nate Colbert was up, but he hit a foul popup to first for the second out of the inning. Kroc later told me he was disappointed, but thought, "Oh well, we still have one more out." Except the runner on first base, 15-year major league veteran Matty Alou, forgot the number of outs and was doubled off to end the inning.

Jack Bloomfield, the Padres' first base coach told me, "I'd just informed Alou to stay on the bag, nowhere to go."

Ray Kroc threw out the first pitch on opening night 1974. The fans loved his comments on the public address system later that night.
From the Bob Chandler collection

Nevertheless, Kroc berated Bloomfield and called him, "My Mute First Base Coach."

"Mr. Kroc, I informed Alou of the situation," Bloomfield replied. "I can't tie a rope around him."

Jack almost lost his job, but remained with the club for the remainder of the year. The same could not be said for Alou. He was immediately sold the next week to a Japanese team.

It seems the only people who really enjoyed Ray's comments were the fans. He was now one of them . . . as frustrated over the team's performance as they were. Kroc vowed future improvement, and the fans continued to buy tickets as fast as they bought his hamburgers. It certainly was a most memorable opening game to raise the curtain on the Ray Kroc regime in San Diego. He saved baseball in San Diego and granted his wish to own a baseball team, but sometimes Kroc must have thought he bought the San Diego Zoo by mistake.

This was the situation when Ray Kroc took the public address microphone. In our radio booth, Jerry Coleman said, "Bob, our new owner is about to speak. Let's see what he has to say."

The crowd hushed, but not for long, as Ray began, "Fans, I suffer with you."

The fans cheered as Kroc continued, "I have some good news and some bad news. The good news is we've outdrawn the Dodgers. They had 31,000 for their opener and we have 39,000 for ours. The bad news is I've never seen such stupid ball playing in my life."

The crowd erupted. The players were stunned. In the broadcast booth, Jerry quickly said, "Let's go to break."

But the excitement of the inning was not over yet. A streaker jumped out of the stands and started sprinting across the outfield. Ray was still holding the microphone and started yelling, "Get that streaker out of here; throw him in jail."

With Ray's words wafting over Mission Valley, the streaker was captured and taken out of sight. The rest of the game was uneventful as Houston won 9-5.

Willie McCovey was the Padres player representative and commented after the game, "I wish Mr. Kroc hadn't done that. I've never heard anything like that in my 19 years in baseball. None of us like being called stupid. We're pros, and we're doing the best we can."

Short-Order Cooks Night

Among those offering commentary for the Houston Astros was Doug Rader. "He [Kroc] thinks he's in a sales convention dealing with a bunch of his short-order cooks."

Kroc contacted McCovey the next day, and the situation was quickly smoothed over, but remember that Ray Kroc was a great merchandiser. The next time Houston came to town, Kroc held a short-order cooks night. Any fan wearing a short-order cook's hat was admitted free. Rader joined in the fun by delivering the Astros starting lineup to the umpires on a platter with a short-order cook's hat atop his head. Coincidence or not, the Padres traded for Rader after the season.

Grinding It Out

In the middle of June, Ray held a book publishing party in Chicago. His book was titled, *Grinding it Out*, the story of Kroc's life and the building of the McDonald's empire. He arranged the release date to coincide with the Padres' first trip to Chicago.

That afternoon at Wrigley Field, a pleased Kroc watched the Padres beat the Cubs 9-4 en route to a three-game series sweep. He hosted a party in his luxurious Lake Shore Drive apartment that evening. It's fair to say most of the movers and shakers in the Chicago sports scene were on hand. Among those in attendance were famous Chicago baseball announcers Harry Caray and Jack Brickhouse, controversial Oakland A's owner Charlie Finley, and the legendary Chicago Bears owner George Halas.

Kroc was in a wonderful mood. He told those assembled, "I'll do everything I can to make our people have pride in this organization. We're going to buy our own jet airplane, stay in better hotels, and do other things that will make people yearn to play for the Padres."

Ray indeed did follow through on most of his promises.

Later in the night, I happened to be within hearing distance as George Halas sidled up to Kroc and said, "Ray, remember when you got on that public address in San Diego on opening day?"

"Certainly I remember that," replied Kroc.

"God, I've always wanted to do that!" exclaimed Halas.

Chapter 8

Spring Training

New Complex

I n 1969, before the final decision was made to choose Yuma, Arizona, as their training site, the Padres actually considered holding spring training in Borrego Springs. Accommodations that first spring in Yuma were a bit sparse. The Padres had just one practice field and played their exhibition games at a glorified high school facility called Keegan Stadium. The home clubhouse was beyond centerfield with outdoor showers. The visitors facilities were located at a municipal stadium about one mile away.

The situation changed dramatically in 1970 as the "Caballeros de Yuma" (a local group of civic-minded citizens) spearheaded a new practice facility that, at the time, was as good as any in baseball. Eventually, it was named the "Ray Kroc Baseball Complex" and had everything a team would need for spring training. There were four playing fields in a clover-leaf design with a huge ultra-modern clubhouse in the center. A chain-link fence surrounded the 25-acre complex. In that first year, the compound was surrounded by nothing but sand. When the desert winds blew, sandstorms were common.

Improvements blossomed each year when the Padres arrived for spring training. Grass replaced the sand around the complex. A convention center was built adjacent to the fields. A municipal golf course opened to the west of the facility. Condos started to appear beyond the outfield fence. A huge landmark water tower was constructed. Tennis courts and a playground were added. Randy Jones

Spring Training in Yuma—(left to right) Jack Murphy, Ray Kroc, Bob Fontaine, Ballard Smith, and Bob Chandler. From the Bob Chandler collection

told me he loved to train in Yuma because, "There was very little to do but concentrate on baseball, and it was a great spot to prepare for the season."

Padres fans found things to do as they frequently drove the three hours from San Diego to Yuma after work on Friday afternoons for a weekend visit. Saturday morning was a good time for golf with an afternoon ballgame at Desert Sun Stadium. When the sun went down, sporting people visited the greyhound track, and others discovered some of the night life in Yuma. Sunday was for sleeping in late, catching the exhibition game in the afternoon, and returning home.

By 1993, the complex was no longer considered state of the art. Much larger and nicer facilities were being constructed in Florida and in the Phoenix area to attract major league teams. Isolated in Yuma from the other teams of the "Cactus League," the Padres finally agreed to move to a new spring training site in the Phoenix suburb of Peoria, Arizona. It's a wonderful place, but now it takes six hours to drive from San Diego. Obviously, not nearly as many Padres fans can see the team in spring training. Yuma will always be a good memory for the old-timers and me.

Herman Levy

For many years, John "Doc" Mattei was the Padres' traveling secretary and the man in charge of spring training. Doc is a character in his own right. He loved to talk about an early employee named Herman Levy who worked at the Brooklyn post office for 36 years and also assisted the Dodgers in various capacities. When the "Bums" moved to Los Angeles in 1958, Herman was left behind to help run Ebbets Field.

"One night they had a big soccer match at Ebbets Field," recalled Mattei. "Herman was parking the cars, and he packed them so tight that there were no aisles to get out or room to move forward or backwards. When the game ended some of the people in front went for dinner or a drink, and nobody could get out. It took four days to get the lot cleared."

Levy was devoted to Mattei and Padre president Buzzie Bavasi. According to Mattei, "Herman once traveled from Vero Beach, Florida, to Los Angeles on a bus to deliver a set of lamps that Bavasi had left behind when the Dodgers ended spring training. Levy carried the lamps to Dodger Stadium, placed them in Bavasi's office, left without a word and boarded a bus back to Brooklyn."

Mattei hired Levy to work for the Padres, and every morning in spring training Herman would raise the American flag over the complex and bellow out the Pledge of Allegiance. Levy was always trying to help people, and everybody liked him.

One spring, the players were confined to their Phoenix hotel by a violent thunderstorm. A number of the Padres were looking for a movie to attend.

"There's one five blocks down the street; you can't miss it," Levy told them.

The players returned 15 minutes later, soaking wet. Levy had failed to inform the players it was a drive-in movie.

During the season, Levy served as the visiting clubhouse attendant at San Diego Stadium. Former Cincinnati Reds pitcher Jack

Billingham recalls the time Levy asked him if there was anything he could do for him.

"Sure," Billingham said, tongue firmly in cheek, "Bring a ham and cheese sandwich down to the bullpen around the sixth inning." When the sixth inning arrived, Levy walked into the Reds' dugout carrying the sandwich.

"What's that?" Cincinnati manager Sparky Anderson demanded.

"The sandwich Billingham asked for," Levy replied innocently.

Anderson wadded the sandwich into a ball and handed it back to Levy. "Take that to Mr. Billingham," he said. "And tell him it cost him $100."

Anderson dropped the fine after Billingham pleaded his case. If he hadn't, Levy would have paid the fine.

In 1977, Levy's big heart finally gave out. He died of a heart attack, and there will never be another Herman Levy.

Pepitone

Brooklyn-born Joe Pepitone was a New York Yankees star during the 1960s, driving in 100 runs in 1964 and hitting as many as 31 homers in 1966. In 1975, he was in spring training camp with the Padres, trying to win a job as a backup first baseman and left-handed pinch hitter.

Joe was actually having a good spring and had a legitimate chance to make the club. Unfortunately, Pepi had a phobia about his pending baldness. To cover his exposed dome, Joe always wore a wig when he went out in public. He even wore it on the baseball diamond.

Late in spring training, Pepitone was playing first base at Desert Sun Stadium, when the batter hit a sharp grounder right at him. Suddenly, the ball took a bad hop toward his head. Joe grabbed his cap to protect his wig instead of going for the ball.

Manager John McNamara released him the next day. Toupee Joe never played in the major leagues again.

What's In a Name?

Left-handed pitcher Bob Owchinko was the Padres' number-one draft choice in June 1976. By 1977, he had already made the big

Bob Chandler interviews Joe Pepitone during spring training. Notice the abundance of hair flowing from beneath Pepi's baseball cap.
From the Bob Chandler collection

league club's starting rotation and the following year posted a 10-13 record, pitching 202 innings with a 3.56 ERA.

It was during spring training in 1979 that Bob pitched in a memorable game without being aware of the significance.

From Japan, the Yakult Swallows shared the Yuma training facility with the Padres for several years. One Sunday, the two clubs played an exhibition game that was televised in both San Diego and Japan.

Other than struggling with the pronunciation of some of the Japanese players' names, the broadcast was routine for the Padres broadcasters.

That was not the case for the Japanese broadcast team. Bob Owchinko became Bob Smith to their TV audience in Japan. In Japanese, Owchinko roughly translates to "little penis"!

Woosh!

During the mid-1980s, while the Padres were still training in Yuma, the team would make several trips back and forth from

Phoenix. It's about a three-hour drive, and although the team provided transportation, many of the players and staff would drive their own cars.

One day, radio producer Tommy Jorgensen and I were cruising back to Yuma from Phoenix at a reasonable 75 miles per hour.

Suddenly, a blur streaked past us traveling at a much higher rate of speed. In a few seconds, we saw a huge cloud of dust appear on the horizon.

It didn't take us long to reach the scene. The car that flew past us was resting against a bush in the highway center divide. A blown tire had spun the vehicle into the divide. The two occupants were badly shaken. The driver was Kurt Bevacqua, and his passenger was Bruce Bochy. Fortunately, neither was injured, but Bochy looked up at us and dead-panned, "Only my cleaner will know for sure."

Revenge Is Sweet

During spring training in 1977, the Padres spent 10 days in the Phoenix area, staying at a downtown hotel called the Central Plaza Inn—a four-story building with players and staff housed on all four levels.

One afternoon, Doug "The Red Rooster" Rader was innocently walking through the courtyard when a player emerged from his room on the fourth level and dumped a bucket of water on Rader. The player (Bobby Valentine) quickly darted back in his room before Rader could see who performed this dastardly deed.

Jerry Coleman and I happened to be walking nearby, and Rader asked, "Who did it?"

"Hear no evil, see no evil, speak no evil," was our response.

"Don't worry," Rader countered. "I'll find out, and there will be a price to pay." Jerry and I had no doubt this would be the case.

The next day, the Padres had a B-squad game scheduled for 10:00 a.m.—with the regular exhibition contest to start at 1:00 p.m. Valentine was in the B-squad game. Jerry and I noticed with suspicion that Rader was lingering near the B-game field even though he was supposed to play in the afternoon.

Valentine was to bat in the first inning, and as he pulled his bat from the rack, a rat seemed to jump out at him. His scream could be heard throughout Phoenix.

Rader had arrived at the field early and killed a rat. He then taped the rodent's tail to the end of Valentine's bat so it would appear to jump at Bobby as he pulled it out of the bat rack.

As Valentine screamed, Rader cackled and moved on to the A-game field. Revenge is sweet.

"My Memory of This Field"

A few years ago, the Padres traveled from Peoria to their original spring training site in Yuma to play an exhibition game. Prior to the contest, I noticed pensive general manager Kevin Towers as he walked by himself to one of the practice fields. I asked his thoughts.

"Bob, in 1985, I was a 23-year-old pitcher in my fourth year with the Padres organization. I was called over to this field to pitch batting practice to the major leaguers. I had pitched the previous season at Double-A Beaumont of the Texas League and figured this was my chance to impress manager Dick Williams and make my jump to the big leagues. Steve Garvey was the hitter, and I decided to show my best stuff. My first pitch was high and inside. My second pitch knocked him down, and my third pitch hit Garvey. That was enough for Williams, and he called for another pitcher. So much for making the team. That's my memory of this field."

Kevin, a high draft choice for the Padres in 1981, was coming off his first full season at Double-A. Control was not his forte. In 160 innings, Towers had surrendered 106 walks.

Garth Brooks

Nationally renowned country singer Garth Brooks spent spring training of 1999 with the Padres in Peoria. Garth is a huge baseball fan, and the Padres thought his presence would generate good publicity. The popular performer also wanted to create awareness for his special "Touch 'Em All" charity.

Brooks played in some games and didn't embarrass himself with his performance. He even got a hit in one game.

At the end of the day, Garth would hang around to sign autographs for as long as people waited in line. The players all liked him, and he showed a strong work ethic, going through all of the drills.

Near the end of spring training, Brooks held a private concert for the players, which I'm told was terrific. Garth told his new teammates that general manager Kevin Towers had offered him "Trevor Hoffman money" to sign.

The singer refused the offer.

"I told Kevin, 'No thanks.' I could make that much money with one concert!"

Trevor had reportedly signed a four-year contract worth in the neighborhood of $30 million.

Nice to Meet You

In mid-March 1998, the Padres were playing an exhibition game at the Peoria Baseball Complex. Ken Caminiti started the game for San Diego and was removed after five innings, which is a normal occurrence during spring training. For the five innings that Cammy played, he endured a true leather-lunged fan who constantly yelled insults at the Padres third baseman. The fan was so loud that we could all hear his venom in the broadcast booth.

Cammy, ever the stoic, never acknowledged the fan. He simply left the game, showered, and dressed. However, instead of heading home, Caminiti returned to the stadium and calmly walked into the stands. He sat down beside the heckler.

"Hi, my name is Ken Caminiti."

Chapter 9

Hang a Star on 1984

The Architect of the 1984 Championship Team

A team's first pennant can be magical, and after 16 seasons of finishing over .500 only once, the 1984 Padres finally won a National League Championship.

The architect of that team was Jack McKeon, who took over as general manager from Bob Fontaine in July 1980. McKeon wanted to start his reconstruction project with a solid young catcher. He identified St. Louis backstop Terry Kennedy as his primary target.

In December 1980, he finally pulled off a deal involving 11 players and got his man. The price was steep. The Padres sent Rollie Fingers, Gene Tenace, Bob Shirley, and young local catching prospect Bob Geren to Whitey Herzog's Cardinals. Along with Kennedy, Whitey forced McKeon to accept six other players (and contracts) that the Redbirds no longer wanted. None stuck with the Padres.

The day after the Kennedy trade, McKeon acquired a sleeper— Alan Wiggins, a young speedster out of the Dodgers organization who didn't attract much attention at the time. Wiggins became an outstanding player in 1984 when he switched to second base, batted leadoff, and stole 70 bases for the Padres.

In April 1981, Trader Jack sent a minor league outfielder to Pittsburgh for minor league southpaw Dave Dravecky. That spring, the Padres and Yankees also exchanged six players with left-handed pitcher Tim Lollar coming to San Diego. Tim had been an All-

America designated hitter at the University of Arkansas and proved to be one of the best-hitting pitchers in Padres history. In addition to being a power threat in the lineup, he won 16 games in 1982 and was an important member of the 1984 staff.

In June of 1981, McKeon supervised a draft that saw outfielders Kevin McReynolds and Tony Gwynn taken with the Padres' first- and third-round picks of the draft. The McReynolds choice was a gamble at the time because he had recently undergone serious knee surgery. Kevin did not play professionally in 1981 but became a minor league star in 1982. He provided power for the '84 Padres. Tony reached the majors in 1982 and won his first batting title with a .351 batting average and 213 hits in 1984.

Enter Dick Williams

Genial giant Frank Howard managed the miserable 1981 Padres. Baseball was on strike for about two months and ended up playing a split schedule. The youthful Padres were painfully consistent. They finished dead last in both splits with an overall 41-69 record. It was not a good fit for either Frank or the Padres. San Diego needed a new manager.

McKeon decided to go for a proven major league manager and brought in Dick Williams as the Padres' new skipper. Williams literally taught the young Padres how to play and more importantly how to win. Under Dick's tutelage, the 1982 and 1983 Padres both finished .500 before their pennant-winning season of '84.

The Wiz For Tempy

In February 1982, the Padres and Cardinals swapped shortstops: Ozzie Smith to St. Louis and Garry Templeton to San Diego. The Padres brain trust decided that, despite Ozzie's brilliant defense, he would never become a good hitter. Templeton, at the time, was one of the best hitting shortstops in baseball, but was conflicting with St. Louis management. The Padres brass was having contractual problems with Ozzie and his agent—so the deal was completed. Ozzie eventually turned into an excellent offensive player and went on to a Hall of Fame career with the Cardinals. Templeton had many good years in San Diego, but a bad knee prevented him from reaching his full potential. However, in 1984, he was a key member of the Padre pennant winners.

Two Bottles of Wine Compliments of Steve Garvey

Following the 1982 season, Dodgers first baseman Steve Garvey became the biggest free agent on the market. After playing 13 seasons for Los Angeles and appearing in eight all-star games, winning the MVP Award in 1974, he was closing in on Billy Williams's NL record for consecutive games played. Steve seemed a perfect fit for the Padres. San Diego president Ballard Smith was making a strong pitch to sign him.

Naturally, Steve and his agent, Jerry Kapstein, were drawing the process out to get the best deal possible. Baseball's winter meetings were held that December in Hawaii. There was wide speculation that Garvey would sign at the meetings.

A career highlight occurred for me one night as I was out for dinner. I noticed a group of Los Angeles sportswriters enjoying their meal at a nearby table. I sent two bottles of wine to their table and told the waiter to say they were compliments of Steve Garvey. The reaction at the table was chaotic until they saw me laughing. Some of those writers still bring that incident up to me.

Garvey finally did sign with the Padres on December 21, 1982, one day before his 34th birthday.

Fly Balls in the Outfield

In December 1983, the Padres, Montreal Expos and Chicago Cubs were involved in a three-team trade that brought power hitter Carmelo Martinez and relief pitcher Craig Lefferts to San Diego. Lefferts turned into an important member of the Padres' 1984 relief corps, and Martinez was switched from first base to left field.

Carmelo was an adequate left fielder, although he once told me during a postgame interview, "Bob, the only thing I don't like about the outfield is the fly balls."

No-nonsense manager Dick Williams taught the young Padres to be winners.
From the San Diego Hall of Champions Collection

Goose and Graig

There were two more key moves to fill out the '84 Padres. In January 1984, the dominant reliever in baseball, Rich "Goose" Gossage, left the Yankees to sign as a free agent with San Diego. He would have 25 saves and 10 wins that year. The closer's role was quite different in those days. Goose frequently worked two or three innings to record his saves.

The blueprint for success was complete with Graig Nettles. The power-hitting, slick-fielding third baseman joined his hometown Padres on March 30, 1984. Left-handed starter Dennis Rasmussen went to the Yankees.

Pivotal backup players Kurt Bevacqua, Bobby Brown, and Champ Summers were signed as free agents. Pitcher Ed Whitson came from Cleveland in a trade while pitchers Andy Hawkins, Eric Show, and Mark Thurmond had been Padre draft picks in the late '70s.

This was a team that Trader Jack built and Dick Williams would mold in his own image. There was much optimism about reaching the playoffs as the Padres began the 1984 season.

A Hot Start

The championship season began with a 5-1 win over Pittsburgh before a sellout crowd of 44,553 at San Diego Stadium. Eric Show worked seven strong innings for the win, and Goose made his Padre debut with two perfect innings of relief. To the delight of the cheering crowd, the Goose struck out the first man he faced on three pitches. In his first at bat, Tony Gwynn doubled a run home. The other two

The Padres signed eight-time All-Star first baseman Steve Garvey in 1982 shown at the press conference with team president Ballard Smith.
From the Bob Chandler collection

young outfielders, Carmelo Martinez and Kevin McReynolds, both homered. Hall of Fame baseball writer Phil Collier called them "The M & M Boys," an allusion to Mickey Mantle and Roger Maris.

The starting lineup for that game remained remarkably consistent throughout the season:

2B	**Wiggins**
RF	**Gwynn**
3B	**Nettles**
1B	**Garvey**
C	**Kennedy**
LF	**Martinez**
CF	**McReynolds**
SS	**Templeton**

The Padres started hot with a 10-2 record, but lost 16 of their next 24 games. The fans began to wonder if this would be just another .500 season.

Re-Ignition

There is an old axiom in baseball that says hitting comes and goes, but speed comes to the ballpark every day. On May 17, Alan Wiggins stole five bases and Tony Gwynn stole two as the Padres snapped a seven-game losing streak with a 5-4 win over Montreal.

When on first base, Wiggins was such a threat to run that Gwynn batted .412.

"I got a lot of fastballs to hit because of Wiggy's threat to steal," remembered Gwynn. "Plus, I had good bat control and could find the holes when the infielders were moving."

The weekend of June 9, the Padres took three straight from Cincinnati and moved back into first place to stay.

Turning Point of the Entire Season

The Padres lost in Los Angeles to the Dodgers 5-4 on June 27, but Dick Williams called the game the turning point of the entire season. Dodger lefthander Fernando Valenzuela struck out 11 and had a three-hit shutout with two outs and nobody on in the ninth.

Suddenly, the Padres put together five hits and a hit batsman against Fernando and reliever Tom Niedenfuer.

Although pinch-hitter McReynolds struck out with runners on first and third to end the game, Williams was adamant. "It pulled us together as a team. Even though we lost, it's the only time all year I've seen our guys celebrate afterward. It was just like we had won."

Despite the defeat, the Padres still led the division by four games.

One of the Key Hits of the Year

San Diego enjoyed a seven-game lead when the team flew into Pittsburgh for a six-game series in July. The Pirates won the first game 5-1 and took the opener of the next day's doubleheader 4-3. John Tudor had a four-hit 1-0 shutout in the nightcap, and the Bucs appeared on the verge of a twin sweep going into the eighth inning. Perhaps it was a good omen when backup catcher Bruce Bochy beat out an infield grounder. In all due respect, it may have been the only infield hit the lead-footed Bochy ever got. With two down, Alan Wiggins beat out another infield chopper, and Tony Gwynn followed with a dramatic three-run homer. The Padres hung on to win 3-2 and split the six games in Pittsburgh. All the players and Dick Williams agreed the homer by Gwynn was one of the key hits of the entire season.

Beanball War in Atlanta

In some 40 years of covering and broadcasting major league baseball, I have seen many beanball wars and fights on the field, but nothing compared to August 12, 1984, in Atlanta, Georgia. The Padres were leading the second-place Braves by 10½ games as the teams prepared for the final game of a four-game series at Fulton County Stadium. It was a good matchup: Ed Whitson (12-5) for the Padres and Pascual Perez (10-4) for Atlanta. Alan Wiggins led off the game for San Diego. On the first pitch, Perez buried a fastball in his ribs. The Padres felt it was a purpose pitch to intimidate them. They spent the rest of the afternoon trying to retaliate.

In the second, Perez was hiding deep in the batter's box, and Whitson brushed him back a couple of times. He went down on strikes, and Terry Kennedy followed him toward the Braves dugout. Perez, bat in hand, raised it as Kennedy approached.

Perez would later say, "I didn't want to fight Kennedy. He had all that gear on, and I raised my bat to protect myself."

Braves reserve Bob Watson grabbed Pascual from behind. "When I saw him ready to take a swing at Kennedy, I had to jump in there. I don't care what team the guy plays for, I'm not going to let anybody get hit with a bat."

Plate umpire Steve Rippley warned both benches. To Rippley's credit, he had allowed Whitson the opportunity to pitch Perez tight. After a warning is issued, if the umpire believes another pitch is intentionally thrown at a batter, the pitcher and his manager are ejected.

In the fourth inning, Eddie Whitson threw three straight inside pitches to Perez. He and Dick Williams were ejected. Two innings later, Jack McKeon's son-in-law, Greg Booker, fired a pitch over Perez' head and was thumbed along with acting manager Ozzie Virgil.

Craig Lefferts, the fourth Padre pitcher of the game, finally nailed Perez in the eighth, inciting a brawl. Perez bolted for the dugout as both teams flooded the field. Padre reserve Champ Summers chased Perez, but a shower of beer and Bob Horner, the Braves' injured third baseman, met him at the steps. Apparently, Horner sensed the escalating tension and left the press box to put on his uniform during the sixth inning. Although the Padres couldn't reach Perez, the situation on the field provided plenty of action. Atlanta's Gerald Perry blindsided Tim Flannery, prompting his ejection along with teammates Rick Mahler and Steve Bedrosian. Lefferts, Summers, acting manager Jack Krol, and Bobby Brown were tossed for San Diego.

However, more fireworks were still to come.

In the ninth inning, Atlanta pitcher Donnie Moore drilled Graig Nettles with his first pitch. Nettles charged the mound to set off another melee. Braves manager Joe Torre, Moore, and Nettles were all banished.

After the game, Joe Torre put the blame on Williams. "He's an idiot with a capital 'I.' I think he should be suspended for the rest of the year."

"You can tell Torre to take that finger he's pointing and stick it," Williams responded.

"Hell . . ." said Kennedy. "If Whit had hit Perez in the second inning the whole thing would've been over, but it took us four damn tries."

Leave it to Kurt Bevacqua to add a little humor to the situation. He was in the middle of both battles and tried to climb into the stands after a fan who had drenched him with a cup of beer.

"I had a great time. Hell, that's the longest I've been on the field in a while."

Flannery, who had given and received his licks said, "I had the time of my life out there. This is a great team, a great bunch of guys. I wouldn't want to play with anyone else. These guys will stand behind you through anything. They talk about chemistry. This is what I call chemistry."

The Braves won the game 5-3 to pull within nine and a half games of the 69-48 Padres, but they never got any closer.

I Got Emotional and Kind of Choked Up

After the Padres clinched and I announced the starting lineup on the radio the next night, I got emotional and kind of choked up. I wasn't expecting it to happen—it just did. I'm guessing after all those years of broadcasting for bad Padre teams, surviving the almost-move to Washington, and remembering just how difficult it had been to bring major league baseball to San Diego, it all bubbled over inside. Actually it was a great feeling, but the best was yet to come.

The team had celebrated late the night before at Goose Gossage's home. Much of the talk at the party concerned Ray Kroc, who had died in January at the age of 84. The team had dedicated the season to him and wore his initials, RAK, on the sleeves of their uniforms. The party livened up when Kroc's widow, Joan, arrived. She was waving her arms and hugging everybody.

"I've been screaming for two solid hours," she said. "We did it; we made it! I'm so excited; this is the greatest!"

Gossage had a swimming pool in his backyard, and eventually, it was time for everyone to get wet. Now, Joan was wearing a very expensive dress, so when some players approached her, she put up her hands.

Mrs. Kroc said, "No."

Then she walked to the edge of the pool . . . and jumped in!

The Goose

The overall value of Goose Gossage cannot be overstated, which is the reason I believe he belongs in the Hall of Fame. Goose was simply the dominant relief pitcher of his era. Why did Dodgers GM Al Campanis think the Padres won the division? His answer was simple:

"Goose. . . . He was the missing part in the puzzle. Without Goose, the Padres are back here with the rest of the division."

Dick Williams felt veterans Gossage and Graig Nettles contributed in other ways.

"Those two used to stay around in that clubhouse after every game and have a few beers and talk to the younger players, getting them thinking baseball and wanting to come to the park. They really put their hearts and souls into it. They got our kids believing."

Two Similar Teams,
But the Cubs Had Sutcliffe

The Padres and Cubs met 12 times during the regular season and split the series 6-6. Cubs outfielder Keith Moreland and Padre manager Dick Williams had similar assessments of the two teams.

"Both ball clubs have put together some pitching, some hitting, some running and some maturity to go along with some raw young talent," Moreland concluded. "I think we're the best two teams in the league. There are a lot of similarities."

"The clubs are built the same way," Williams concurred. "They probably outpower us, maybe because of their ballpark. I know we outdefense them, and we have better speed. The pitching is pretty even."

However, most pundits predicted a Cubs NL Championship because of one man: Rick Sutcliffe. Chicago had acquired the towering right-hander from Cleveland in June. He was 4-5 for the Tribe, but a change of venue made him into the most dominant pitcher in baseball. Rick went 16-1 with the Cubs. On the Fourth of July, he beat the Padres 2-1 before over 52,000 fans at San Diego Stadium. During the regular season, he had two wins against San Diego.

The Cubs Were Stealing Signs on TV

The Cubs also had another advantage. They were stealing opposing catchers' signs deep within the friendly confines of Wrigley Field. Veteran players would go inside the clubhouse and watch the television monitor because the centerfield camera covered home plate on every pitch. When a Cubs player reached second base, he would relay the catcher's signs to the batter. How much this helped during the '84 season is a matter of conjecture. It certainly didn't hurt.

"We Are Going to Slaughter Those Lousy Wimps"

The first day of the playoffs, a column in the *Chicago Tribune* by the great scribe Mike Royko poked fun at San Diego and the Southern California lifestyle. Some excerpts:

"The fact is, in San Diego they're not obsessed. They aren't delirious with the drama and historical significance of the playoffs. It's just another pleasant, recreational diversion.

San Diego mayor Roger Hedgecock welcomes Goose Gossage to town.
From the Bob Chandler collection

"They have no sense of tradition because they have no tradition.

"Even their ball park is disgusting. It's new [ed. note: remember this was 1984] and modern and clean. And the fans wouldn't even think of getting in brawls or cursing an opponent or tossing beer on an outfielder. Instead, they come to the park in the skimpiest of clothing and admire one another's nautilus-tuned bods. And anybody with a manly, bleacher-bum belly is viewed as an affront to the environment.

"But I'm not worried about San Diego winning. That's because I truly believe that there is fairness and equity in life. And in truth, justice and the American way. And because we have fairness, equity, truth, justice, and the American way on our side, we are going to slaughter those lousy wimps."

Royko The Genius

Royko looked like a genius after the first game. On the first pitch of the game, Padres starter Eric Show thought he threw a perfect strike to leadoff hitter Bob Dernier. It was called a ball by a replacement umpire. Show's second pitch sailed over the ivy-covered wall for a homer. Sutcliffe pitched seven innings of two-hit shutout ball and even hit a home run. Gary Matthews added two more homers, and the Cubs waltzed to a 13-0 win before a delirious Chicago crowd.

The second game was more competitive, but the result was the same. The Cubs won 4-2 to take a commanding two-game lead in the best-of-five series. It was off to San Diego for Game 3 the next day.

To add insult to injury, the Padres flight was delayed. While we all sat in the plane waiting for take-off, the Cubs' charter was cleared for departure. It was a somber flight back to San Diego. If I've ever seen a defeated team, it was the Padres on that airplane. Players were discussing their off-season plans.

Thousands of Loyal Fans
Welcome the Padres Home

Our charter flight landed on an obscure runway at Lindbergh Field. Only a few people waited near the busses that would transport us to San Diego Stadium. A player said that was all they deserved after the two games in Chicago.

Then en route to the stadium on Friars Road, we heard the driver talking about an alternative route because of the crowds waiting to greet the team. Because of the delay getting out of Chicago, a jubilant, party-ready throng of several thousand had migrated to the parking lot.

In all my years with major league baseball, I have never seen the mood of a team change as radically as when the Padres saw this reception. The team came out and was surrounded by cheering fans. Dick Williams got on a scooter and zipped around shaking hands and talking to everybody. Meanwhile, the players were high-fiving their loyal fans. It was an unexpected welcome home.

I heard one player complain about the crowd because he wanted to get to his car. Reserve Bobby Brown told him to enjoy this moment because he might never get to the playoffs again. To his credit, the player stood for a moment and then went to slap some skin. In a few minutes, he was totally involved in the celebration.

Incidentally, he never did make the playoffs again. . . .

A Comeback for the Ages

A sellout crowd of 58,346 showed up for San Diego's first-ever home playoff game. They were extremely loud. During pregame introductions, the normally reticent Garry Templeton took off his cap and waved it to the crowd. The place went wild. Larry Bowa, in his final years as a player, was the Cubs shortstop. He later told me that when he saw the crowd reaction and heard the deafening noise, he started to get concerned.

Although Templeton's cap waving stirred the masses, his leaping catch that saved a run in the first inning and his two-run double in the fifth giving the Padres the lead were more tangible contributions to victory. Ed Whitson pitched eight innings and allowed just one run. Kevin McReynolds wrapped up the game with a three-run homer. The Padres recorded their first playoff victory by a score of 7-1.

Garvey's Greatest Game

Following an off day, Game 4 was played before another raucous sell-out Saturday evening crowd. It turned out to be a classic. Rick Sutcliffe was slotted to pitch, but Cubs manager Jim Frey elected to save him for the first game of the World Series or a deciding fifth game of the playoffs, if needed. Scot Sanderson started for Chicago. Tim Lollar took the mound for San Diego. Neither pitcher would be around at the end.

The Padres jumped to an early 2-0 lead on Steve Garvey's two-out, two-run double in the third—the start of a memorable day for the Garv. Chicago took the lead 3-2 in the fourth on back-to-back home runs by Jody Davis and Leon Durham. The Padres knotted the game in the fifth on Garvey's two-out single. A passed ball and another two-out single by Garvey put the Padres on top 5-3 in the seventh. The Cubs tied the score 5-5 in the eighth with a big double by Jody Davis. The bases were loaded in the top of the ninth when Craig Lefferts retired Ron Cey on a ground out. The game moved to the bottom of the inning with Cubs relief ace Lee Smith fresh from the bullpen.

I was standing at the end of the Padres dugout waiting to do my postgame interview. I remember commenting to several members of the media that no matter who won, it had been a terrific game. It was about to get better. Tony Gwynn singled with one out, bringing Garvey to the plate. Garvey had dislocated a thumb in July of 1983 which still affected his power swing in 1984. Steve had only hit eight homers all year, his last on August 15.

Lee Smith had an outstanding fastball which he threw to Garvey, up and away. Steve swung and completed his marvelous night with a walkoff home run over the right field wall. The Padres had won the game 7-5; Garvey had driven in five runs. The series was deadlocked two apiece.

Pandemonium reigned.

Tony Gwynn called Garvey's clutch hitting the greatest one-game performance he'd ever seen. The only negative occurred when Kevin McReynolds slid into second base trying to break up a double play. Unfortunately, what he broke was a bone in his right wrist. Kevin was lost for the rest of the postseason—the only serious injury the Padres had suffered all year.

The Fifth and Deciding Game

For the fifth and deciding game, the Cubs had the well-rested Sutcliffe to start against the Padres' Eric Show. Whether the extra day of rest had any effect on their ace, we'll never know. Show was knocked out of the game in the second inning after serving up home runs to Leon Durham and Jody Davis that gave Chicago a 3-0 lead. Meanwhile, Sutcliffe was brilliant through five innings. The Padres mustered only two hits. No base runner had reached second base. However, after the second inning, a Padre bullpen of Andy Hawkins, Dave Dravecky, Craig Lefferts, and Goose Gossage came in to shut down the Cubs on two hits.

In the Padres' sixth, the crowd began to get into the game again. The noise grew louder as Alan Wiggins reached first on a bunt. Gwynn followed with a single. Garvey walked to load the bases. Graig Nettles and Terry Kennedy followed with sacrifice flies. The Cubs lead was cut to 3-2. Davey Lopes was a veteran utility player on that Cubs team. He recognized Sutcliffe was losing something off his fastball. Lopes told me he hoped manager Jim Frey would choose pragmatism over loyalty. Lefty Steve Trout was ready to face San Diego's left-handed hitters, but Sutcliffe was Frey's horse. He had gone 16-1 for his manager during the regular season and dominated the first game of the playoffs. Sutcliffe had only allowed the Padres a pair of runs in 13 innings of playoff pitching. The big man went to the mound to start the seventh inning.

Carmelo Martinez worked him for a walk and was sacrificed to second by Templeton. Tim Flannery batted for Lefferts. Tim hit a ground ball that went right through the legs of first baseman Leon Durham. Martinez scored the tying run. It has been said that this play cost the Cubs the title. I disagree. Martinez would have been at third with two outs. When Wiggins came through with a single to left, Carmelo would have scored.

Gwynn was the batter—in my view, this was the key to the game. Tony ripped a ball that shot past second baseman Ryne Sandberg. It was hit so hard it rolled to the fence, and two runs came in to put the Padres on top 5-3.

Steve Garvey hit the most famous home run in Padres history to beat the Chicago Cubs 7-5 in Game 4 of the 1984 NL Playoffs.
From the Bob Chandler collection

"At the time I felt it was the hardest ball I'd ever hit," recalled Gwynn. "The crowd noise was so loud, I couldn't even hear third base coach Ozzie Virgil."

Garvey followed with another hit scoring Gwynn to make it 6-3, San Diego. Goose polished off the last two innings, and San Diego was in the World Series for the first time.

Pick Your Champagne

Padres owner Joan Kroc always went first class. She ordered 40 bottles of expensive "Dom Perignon" champagne for the players. Savvy traveling secretary Doc Mattei knew the champagne would be used for spraying and not for drinking. Mattei had one of the clubhouse boys purchase 40 bottles of the cheapest champagne he could find for the clubhouse celebration. The next day, he placed a bottle of Dom Perignon in each player's locker for their future consumption.

Forty More Years! Forty More Years!

Simply stated, the citizens of San Diego went wild after the game. Their chant was, "Forty more years! Forty more years!" in reference to the Cubs' last appearance in the World Series. Along the freeways, from the mesa tops, echoing through the suburban areas, and especially in the beach districts, fans blared their horns loud and long. They wanted Mike Royko to hear them all the way in Chicago. Several thousand fans blocked streets in South Mission, guzzling beer and screaming in delight. Thousands more turned out to celebrate along Mission Beach and Pacific Beach. A rock band played on the beach as fans gathered around bonfires. Grocers reported selling more champagne than on New Year's Eve. Two police officers at the beach scene said they saw no cause to move in to clear the fans out, noting, "This is just a big party."

The party lasted deep into the night and extended all the way to Green Bay, Wisconsin, where the Chargers defeated the Packers 34-28. Ray Preston, a linebacker on the Chargers, told me that players were jumping up and down on the sideline when they heard the score from San Diego. I can imagine what the Packer fans were thinking. It truly was a celebration to long savor and remember in San Diego.

Bring on the Tigers

On to the World Series against a very powerful Detroit Tigers team. Motown had wrapped up the AL Eastern Division early after an incredible 35-5 run to start the season. The Tigers were led by money pitcher Jack Morris, superb closer Willie Hernandez, catcher Lance Parrish, intense Kirk Gibson and San Diego's own Alan Trammell.

In the '84 series, the DH was used in all games. San Diego appointed Kurt Bevacqua as their main designated hitter. The oddsmakers made Detroit 8-5 favorites.

In the first game, Terry Kennedy's two-run double put San Diego up 2-1 in the first inning. The lead lasted until Larry Herndon hit a two-run homer off Padres starter Mark Thurmond in the fifth. The key play of the game occurred when Bevacqua led off the seventh with a shot down the right field line. It appeared Kurt had a triple, but he stumbled between second and third base. He was gunned down in a close play at third. The Padres never threatened again. Jack Morris pitched a 3-2 complete-game victory.

Game 2 did not begin with promise for the Padres. Starting pitcher Ed Whitson was knocked out in the first after allowing three runs—the only runs the Tigers would score. Brilliant relief work by Andy Hawkins and Craig Lefferts blanked Detroit on two hits over the next eight and one-third innings. Trailing 3-2 in the fifth, the Padres put two runners on base with mighty Kurt Bevacqua advancing to the bat. Primarily a line-drive hitter, Kurt lined one into the left field seats for a three-run shot. The Padres held on for the 5-3 win. Bevacqua pirouetted around the bases, waving his arms and blowing kisses to the crowd. It would be the only World Series win in San Diego history.

Detroit controlled the next three games at Tiger Stadium. The series was over, but the fireworks were just beginning.

What Might Have Happened Had the Tigers Lost?

Expecting a riotous celebration, Detroit officials discretely removed San Diego mayor Roger Hedgecock, team wives and officials in the seventh inning of the deciding game. They were in the airport bar watching the conclusion on television. What they saw were thousands of Tiger fans jumping on the field. A few of the revelers suffered leg injuries. Others grabbed chunks of turf and threw them at the broadcast booth which was located closer to the field than at any other stadium. We quickly closed the window. Outside the park, the celebrants thought it would be fun to turn over a taxicab and set it on fire. Not satisfied, the unruly crowd graduated to torching a police car. Before the carnage was over, 80 people were injured, there was one death and 34 arrests. In the morning, the streets were littered with burnt-out vehicles and broken glass.

Padres players, coaches, support people and media were escorted to two busses for the ride to the airport. Bottles and other forms of debris were thrown at them. A few drunks tried to climb aboard while others rocked the large motor coaches back and forth. The mood was tense.

"Some players were terrified," remembered Gwynn. "There were a few of them crying. To be honest, I was as scared as I've ever been."

The busses could not move. Eventually, mounted police, riding side by side, came down the street swinging billy clubs to clear a path. Slowly, we headed for the airport. One could only imagine what might have happened had the Tigers *lost* the World Series.

Chapter 10

Three Frustrating Seasons

The Most Frustrating Season

The Padres' most frustrating season? Easy: 1985. With a pennant-winning lineup in place, the brass determined that a dominant starting pitcher was all the team needed to repeat.

In December 1984, they got their "horse." LaMarr Hoyt came from the Chicago White Sox for Tim Lollar, Luis Salazar, and a promising young shortstop prospect named Ozzie Guillen. The Padres knew Guillen would be a good major league shortstop, but he was behind Garry Templeton. It seemed like a good decision at the time.

In January, the Padres signed two free agents: infielder Jerry Royster from Atlanta and relief pitcher Tim Stoddard from the Chicago Cubs. Backup outfielder Al Bumbry was added in March. Hoyt joined Dave Dravecky, Andy Hawkins, Eric Show, and Mark Thurmond as five first-rate starters. Goose Gossage and Craig Lefferts would still head the bullpen.

Wiggins's Drug Problems

On April 28, Tony Gwynn homered in the ninth off Fernando Valenzuela as the Padres beat Los Angeles 1-0 at Dodgers Stadium and moved into first place with a 10-8 record.

However, an incident that occurred three days earlier caused irreparable damage to the Padres' pennant chances. Alan Wiggins failed to show up for the April 25 game and disappeared for two days. Later found high on drugs, he would never play for the Padres again. It was not his first drug offense, and Joan Kroc immediately ordered him traded. He went to Baltimore, and the Padres were never able to duplicate his speed at the top of the order.

"When Wiggins left it changed the whole personality of the team," remembered Gwynn. "We lost our leadoff hitter, and I didn't get as many fastballs. I began to wonder if I was as good as I thought I was. Plus, there was a lot of dissension between the pro-Wiggins group of players and the anti-Wiggins group. We actually had the same dissension in 1984, but the team was winning, which pushed everything else to the background. When the 1985 team started losing, the dissension became a bigger issue."

The Padres replaced him at second base with a combination of Tim Flannery and Jerry Royster. They became known as "Timry Flanster" and actually did a good job. Both batted .281, combined to score 81 runs, but together stole just eight bases. The Padres were just not the same offensive machine without the speedy Wiggins leading the way.

Padres Dominate The All-Star Game

The Padres remained in first place as late as the Fourth of July and maintained a five-game lead until the bubble burst. San Diego lost eight of their next 11 going into the All-Star break and dropped a half game behind the Dodgers on July 14.

Regardless, the 1985 All-Star game at Minnesota was a Padres showcase. San Diego skipper Dick Williams managed the Nationals to a 6-1 triumph over the American League, using seven of his players, five of whom started the game. LaMarr Hoyt, the starting pitcher, got the win and was voted the game MVP. His catcher, Terry Kennedy, drove in a run with a single. Steve Garvey started at first base and singled home a run. Third baseman Graig Nettles and right fielder Tony Gwynn also started for the National League. Reserve Garry Templeton contributed a pinch-hit single, and Goose Gossage struck out two batters in the final inning.

There's a story about how Hoyt was named the starting pitcher. Just before the break, the Padres faced the Cardinals in St. Louis.

Joaquin Andujar had a 15-3 record for the Cards. The St. Louis media was pushing for him to start the All-Star game, and Dick Williams knew Andujar had a volatile personality. Williams also knew he'd pitch against the Padres in the series. The manager publicly announced he had not yet made a decision on his starting pitcher. This infuriated Andujar who proclaimed he would not, under any circumstances, start the game. The Padres and La Marr Hoyt beat Andujar and the Cardinals 2-0, so Hoyt got the nod. With seven shutout innings against the Redbirds, he improved his record to 12-4. Williams's psychology may have helped the Padres defeat Andujar and open the door for Hoyt. The temperamental Andujar faded and finished the season 21-12, fourth in the Cy Young balloting for 1985. The Padres also faded in 1985 and dropped into a third place tie with Houston in the NL West with a record of 83-79.

Bulge Where?

A downward spiral began in 1986 for LaMarr Hoyt. While his record slipped to 8-11—the least of his worries—the burly right-hander had three drug-related incidents with law enforcement in a nine-month period. Finally, on October 28, 1986, customs officials busted Hoyt at the San Ysidro border with 500 illegal pills in his possession (mostly sedatives).

The next morning's headline read: "LaMarr Hoyt arrested at border with suspicious bulge in groin area."

You can figure out where the pills were hidden. Hoyt never pitched in the majors again.

1989

One of the most interesting seasons in Padres history was 1989. The previous year, on June 28, 1988, the Padres were 10 games under .500 with a 46-56 record. The rest of the way, the team went 15 games over .500 with a 37-22 mark and finished strong at 83-78. In the off-season, slugger Jack Clark came from the New York Yankees. Pitcher Bruce Hurst left Boston to sign a free agent deal on December 8. Optimism ran high as the 1989 season opened.

The Padres began by losing two straight to the Giants with Hurst giving up eight runs in his debut. Six days later against the Atlanta

Braves, Hurst walked pitcher Pete Smith and surrendered a two-run homer to Lonnie Smith on an 0-2 pitch. They were the only walk and hit he allowed. Hurst faced 29 batters and struck out 13 as the Padres won 5-2. In June, popular John Kruk and Randy Ready were traded to Philadelphia for outfielder Chris James, who proved to be a tough, inspirational leader down the stretch. Little Leon "Bip" Roberts provided offensive spark (.301), 21 stolen bases and defensive versatility.

However, by July 23, the team had dropped 11½ games behind the San Francisco Giants with a 47-52 record. Then from July 25 until the end of the season, the Padres ignited (42-21) and frantically chased the Giants. On August 9, the Padres called up pitcher Andy Benes from the minors. Benes had been baseball's number-one draft choice in June of 1988. His first game against Atlanta was rocky, but Benes finished the season with a 6-3 record in 10 starts.

Padres Go On a 17-3 Tear

The Padres won a pair and finally climbed to .500 on August 25 (64-64), still trailing the Giants by nine games. They continued hot, taking 17 of 20, and by September 12 had pulled within five games of San Francisco with a 79-67 record.

On August 31, the Padres traded Luis Salazar and Marvell Wynne to the Chicago Cubs for outfielder Darrin Jackson and pitcher Calvin Schiraldi. Jackson solidified center field and Schiraldi aided the bullpen, with one notable exception in September during crunch time.

Wynne had not helped himself when the Padres lost the first game of an August 11 doubleheader to Atlanta 6-5. In the bottom of the ninth, pinch hitter Wynne singled to center and was sacrificed to second by Bip Roberts. Robby Alomar and Tony Gwynn were the next scheduled hitters. Unfortunately, they never had a chance to drive in the tying run because Wynne fell victim to the old hidden ball trick. Jeff Treadway tagged him out while he stood off second base. Ted Leitner and I were broadcasting the game on cable, and to this day, I still marvel at the stunned look on poor Marvell's face.

The regular season would end with the Padres hosting the Giants for a three-game series at Jack Murphy Stadium. Obviously, to have a chance to catch San Francisco, the Padres would have to be trailing by three games or less when the series began.

Four Games Out with Four Games to Go

On September 26, the Padres beat Cincinnati 3-1; the Giants lost. The Padres had closed to four, and only one game remained before the Giants' series.

The Giants lost again on September 27. The Padres would move within three games if they again defeated a mediocre Cincinnati team. The Reds (73-85) got terrific pitching that day and led 1-0 going into the Padres' ninth. Roberts and Alomar singled, then Gwynn sacrificed the runners to second and third. An intentional pass to Jack Clark loaded the bases. Chris James grounded to short, but the only play the Reds had was at first. With the score tied 1-1, the Padres filled the bases again. Reliever John Franco fanned Benito Santiago to end the inning.

The Reds loaded the bases with two out in the 10th, but failed to score. The Padres loaded the bases with one out in the 11th and failed to score.

In the 13th inning, Calvin Schiraldi took the mound for San Diego. Herm Winningham led off with a single and stole second. Schiraldi retired the next two Reds, bringing superstar Eric Davis to the plate. Davis had 34 homers and 100 RBIs, but was a right-handed batter. The choice was either pitch to Davis or intentionally walk him to face Todd Benzinger. Benzinger, a switch hitter, would bat left-handed against Schiraldi. Benzinger was hitting .244 with 17 homers and 76 RBIs.

Padres manager Jack McKeon let Schiraldi choose who he would rather face. Schiraldi made a fatal decision. Davis missed a home run by inches as he lined one high off the fence in left-center field. The Reds led 2-1. For the record, Benzinger then flied out to center.

The Padres had one last chance in the bottom of the 13th. Tony Gwynn singled and got sacrificed to second. Reds relief pitcher Norm Charlton retired James and Templeton to end the game. Cincinnati won 2-1 in 13 innings.

Tony Captures Third Batting Crown on the Last Day

The Padres dropped to four games behind San Francisco with three games to go. The race was over. The Giants were the 1989 Western Division champions.

There was still individual drama as Giants first baseman Will Clark and Tony Gwynn were neck and neck for the batting title. Clark entered into the series with a .333 average; Tony was on his heels at .332. Clark went two-for-four in the first game, while Tony was one-for-five. Clark increased his lead .334 to .331. In game two, Clark was one-for-four; Tony went three-for-four. It was Clark .334 and Gwynn .333 with one game left.

On the final day, Clark got one hit in four at-bats. Reminiscent of Ted Williams in 1941, Tony responded with another three-for-four game to wrestle away the batting title. Gwynn captured his third-straight batting championship with a .336 average but said he would have gladly traded the batting crown for the division title.

Besides Gwynn, Robby Alomar came into his own at second base, batting .295 with 42 stolen bases. Chris James had 11 homers with 46 RBIs in half a season. Jack Clark powered 26 homers with 94 RBIs, and Benito Santiago was a superb catcher with 16 home runs and 62 RBIs. Pitching-wise, Hurst finished 15-11, 2.69. Ed Whitson was 16-11 (2.66), and Mark Grant had a good year out of the bullpen, going 8-2 (3.33) with two saves in 50 games.

However, the big star in the bullpen was lefthander Mark Davis.

Mark Davis Wins the Cy Young

Mark Davis won the Cy Young Award by appearing in 70 games with a 4-3 record, 1.85 ERA, and 44 saves in 48 chances. Davis threw a great breaking ball in 1989 and averaged a strikeout an inning while giving up just 66 hits in 93 innings of work.

Two of his four blown saves came in one series at Houston. The blown save on June 6 should go in *Ripley's Believe It or Not*. The Padres led the Astros 7-4 going into the bottom of the ninth at the Astrodome. Davis quickly retired the first two batters before Billy Doran singled to left. During the season, Davis averaged one walk every three innings, but inexplicably he suddenly lost control. Mark walked four straight, forcing two runs across, and the score was now 7-6 Padres. The Astros had the bases loaded, two outs and light-hitting catcher Alex Trevino at the plate. Davis struck out Trevino with a sharp breaking ball to apparently end the game. The pitch bounced about six feet away from Padres catcher Benito Santiago. All Santiago had to do was pick up the ball and tag home plate to seal the Padres victory. Instead, Benito tried to tag the man coming home from third base. The runner knocked the ball out of Santiago's hand and scored the tying run. The Astros ended up winning 8-7 in 10 innings.

Who was the aggressive runner who knocked the ball out of Santiago's hand? It was Houston third baseman, Ken Caminiti!

"You Learn Somthing New Every Day, Man"

Following the game, Santiago was asked, "Why didn't you just touch home plate?"

He didn't know he could and added, "You learn something new every day, man."

Billy Doran, who started the tying rally, understated the obvious, "Something like this won't happen again for 100 years."

Padres manager Jack McKeon, in baseball for over 50 years, said it all with, "I've seen it all now." Nevertheless, August and September were thrilling for Padres fans. The team won 42 of their final 63 games, and optimism ran high again for 1990.

Laying an Egg in 1990

After broadcasting Padres games for over 30 years, I believe the worst seasons are when you feel the team is really good and lays an egg instead.

McKeon felt he could win the pennant in 1990 with one more power hitter in the lineup. Joe Carter in Cleveland was the man he targeted. Jack offered the Indians their choice of two talented young catchers in Benito Santiago and Sandy Alomar, Jr. The Tribe selected Alomar. They also wanted outfielder Chris James and minor league infielder Carlos Baerga. The Padres' minor league staff begged Jack not to trade Baerga, a switch-hitting infielder from Puerto Rico who could run and had some power. Jack said he was not going to let a player who wouldn't help the Padres for a couple of years stand in the way of making the deal. The trade was completed, and the Padres got Carter. Alomar and Baerga turned into All-Stars for Cleveland, while the 1990 Padres missed the enthusiasm and competitiveness of James.

Another major setback occurred when Mark Davis turned down the Padres' final offer and signed a lucrative deal with the Kansas City Royals. Davis, a bust in Kansas City, never again came close to achieving what he had done with the Padres in 1989. We'll never know what might have happened had he stayed with San Diego. To replace Davis, McKeon signed former Padre Craig Lefferts. Lefferts did a good job in 1990, but his 23 saves fell far short of what Davis had done for the club in 1989.

McKeon also brought in outfielder Fred Lynn, who had been a great player in Boston, California, and Baltimore. Jack felt Lynn's experience and left-handed bat would provide needed experience and leadership for the Padres.

Good on Paper

The opening day lineup against the Dodgers on April 9, 1990, looked good on paper:

3B	**Bip Roberts**
2B	**Roberto Alomar**
RF	**Tony Gwynn**
1B	**Jack Clark**
CF	**Joe Carter**
LF	**Fred Lynn**
C	**Benito Santiago**
SS	**Garry Templeton**
P	**Bruce Hurst**

Bip Roberts and Robby Alomar were productive hitters with excellent speed. Gwynn, a great hitter with plus speed, stole 40 bases in 1989. Clark, Carter, Lynn, and Santiago all had plus power, and savvy veteran Templeton drove in 59 runs in 1990.

However, the 1990 Padres never clicked. To begin with, they didn't get along well with each other. Especially at odds were two of the team's biggest stars, Jack Clark and Tony Gwynn. Clark felt Gwynn was a selfish player, and a team meeting was called when the club was in New York. Gwynn remembered Clark starting the meeting by throwing a cup of root beer across the clubhouse. Mark Grant was there and confirmed the cup exploded when it hit between his legs.

Clark pointed his finger at Gwynn, and said, "You're the problem on this team; you're a selfish son of a bitch!"

Gwynn had other ideas and admitted, "I said some things to Jack I probably shouldn't have."

Soon, they were nose to nose, and a fight almost ensued. It's Tony's opinion that Clark felt Gwynn received too much attention for a player who was not a "game changer." Clark objected to Gwynn dragging a bunt when runners were on first and second and nobody out. It was Jack's opinion that Gwynn was trying to protect his batting average by either getting a bunt single or credit for a sacrifice. Tony felt he was helping the team by advancing the runners for the "game changers"—Jack Clark and Joe Carter. Gwynn was simply playing the Dick Williams/Jack McKeon style of baseball.

Nevertheless, for the rest of the season, Gwynn never bunted in that situation again. He tried to drive the ball and saw his batting average drop to .309 even though he drove in 10 more runs than in 1989.

The bickering Padres last saw .500 on June 28 when the team was 35-35, 10 games behind Cincinnati. Jack McKeon was replaced as field manager by Greg Riddoch at the All-Star break. The team's performance failed to improve. By July 23, the Padres were 38-54, 21 games out of first place. San Diego went on an impressive 16-5 run to improve to a 54-59 on August 12, but still remained 11½ games behind the Reds.

In His Wildest Dreams

The Padres finished with a 21-28 stretch run and final record of 75-87—16 games behind Cincinnati. The season had turned into a rotten egg.

None of the key Padres had a special year. Even Gwynn batted just .309, low for him. Jack Clark hit 25 home runs but missed 47 games with injuries. Carter, a terrific person, played in every game, but batted just .232. He connected for 24 homers with 115 RBIs. Ed Whitson was the top starter with a 14-9 record; Hurst just 11-9 and Benes 10-11.

It was around this time that I asked Greg Riddoch if, in his wildest dreams, he could imagine the 1990 Padres having this kind of season. Greg responded, "In my wildest dreams, baseball never entered the picture. . . ."

Chapter 11

The Most Exciting Season in Franchise History

1996

The 1996 regular season was probably the most exciting in franchise history. The Padres were never more than two and a half games out of first place and captured the division in dramatic Hollywood style on the final day of the season in Los Angeles.

First, we must backtrack to set the stage. As a result of the notorious "fire sale," the 1993 Padres were a disaster and struggled through a devastating 61-101 season. Most of the team's best players were sold or traded because the franchise was in serious financial trouble. By mid-August of the following year, the hapless Padres were stumbling along at 47-70, when the major league players voted to go on strike. The World Series was cancelled, and players were still on the picket line when a stranger from Houston named John Moores purchased the team in December 1994. His first hire as president and chief executive officer was Larry Lucchino. San Diego immediately pulled the trigger on a major trade with the Astros that brought Steve Finley and Ken Caminiti to Mission Valley. The revitalized Padres of 1995 were part of the pennant race into September, but finished 70-74, eight games out of first.

Hope was high for 1996.

Good Moves

Veteran left-hander Fernando Valenzuela, thought to be over the hill, had been signed as a free agent in 1995. The Padres were hopeful the former Dodgers icon would attract new fans from below the border. Fernando responded with an 8-3 record. In 1996, he started 31 games and posted a 13-8 record.

Another veteran pitcher, right-hander Bob Tewksbury, signed a free-agent contract and went 10-10 with a memorable start in the season's final game.

First baseman Wally Joyner was acquired from Kansas City and provided outstanding defense to go with a .277 batting average and 65 RBIs. His leadership was a stabilizing factor.

Baseball's all-time best leadoff hitter, Rickey Henderson, joined the Padres as a free agent and contributed 37 stolen bases, a .410 on-base percentage, and a positive, fun-loving influence in the clubhouse.

Tony's younger brother, Chris Gwynn, came to spring training on a minor league contract, made the team, and provided the season's most dramatic pinch-hit on the final day of the regular season.

The Padres' opening-day lineup April 1 at Wrigley Field in Chicago looked like this:

LF	Rickey Henderson
CF	Steve Finley
RF	Tony Gwynn
3B	Ken Caminiti
1B	Wally Joyner
C	Brad Ausmus
SS	Andujar Cedeno
2B	Jody Reed

This lineup helped the Padres begin the season 35-20, the best 55-game start in franchise history. The Padres led the division by six and a half games, and everything appeared rosy.

"Rickey Don't Have Ten Year"

Early in the season, as the players rode the bus to the ballpark, Tony Gwynn was seated in the front row as the senior member of the team. Usually the veteran players sit up front while the rookies and younger players are in the back of the bus. On this ride, Rickey Henderson was sitting in the back, when Tony called out, "Rickey, sit up front. You have tenure."

Henderson replied, "No, no, Rickey don't have 10 year; Rickey has 17 year."

The bus exploded with laughter. Life was good.

June Gloom

In early June, the Padres were trying to sweep a three-game series at Philadelphia. Trailing 8-5 going into the ninth, Steve Finley tied the game with a dramatic three-run homer. Unfortunately, the magic evaporated, and the Phillies rebounded to win 9-8 in 12 innings. To make matters worse, Wally Joyner broke his left thumb trying to break up a double play and was lost to the team until July 11. Coincidence or not, the Padres dropped 19 of their next 23 games. On June 26, they stood 39-39—two games out of first place.

General manager Kevin Towers felt the team needed a shakeup and pulled off a mid-June trade with the Detroit Tigers. Outstanding defensive catcher Brad Ausmus and erratic shortstop Andujar Cedeno

Rickey Henderson slides back into first base.
From the San Diego Hall of Champions Collection

went to Detroit for catcher John Flaherty and shortstop Chris Gomez.

The trade paid immediate dividends for San Diego. Flaherty's longest hitting streak during five seasons in the American League was six games. From June 21 through July 27, he hit safely in 27 consecutive games. It was the second longest hitting streak in San Diego history, surpassed only by Benito Santiago's 34 consecutive-game record in 1987. Incidentally, Tony Gwynn's longest hitting streak was 25 games.

Greg Vaughn Arrives

From June 27 to the end of July, the Padres went 19-12 for a 58-51 mark and a half-game lead over the Dodgers. Towers attempted to further strengthen the team for the stretch run by acquiring power-hitting left fielder Greg Vaughn from Milwaukee. When Vaughn joined the Padres, he was batting .280 with 31 homers and 95 RBIs in just 102 games for the Brewers. From that time on, Greg was a disappointment for the Padres, batting .206 with 10 homers and 22 RBIs in 43 games. Two years later, he would more than make up for his late-season slump in 1996.

The addition of Vaughn did create a problem in the outfield. Tony Gwynn and Steve Finley were set in right field and center field. Vaughn would play ahead of Rickey Henderson in left field. This caused a ticklish balancing act for manager Bruce Bochy.

"I tried to solve the problem with straight-on communication," recalled Bochy. "I told each of them I was in a tough spot and would get both of them playing time."

Bruce remembered Henderson saying, "Rickey is okay with this as long as Rickey knows when Rickey is going to play."

A Legend Created

The month of August belonged to Ken Caminiti. He was unstoppable. Cammy belted 14 homers and drove in 38 runs during the span of 28 games. A legend was created on August 18 while the Padres were playing the New York Mets in Monterrey, Mexico. I was announcing the game on radio with Ted Leitner. Ted had just come from the Padres clubhouse bearing news that Caminiti was on the training table with an IV in his arm. Cammy had been sick and was severely dehydrated. Bruce Bochy later said Caminiti looked as bad as any player he'd ever seen.

He told him, "No way you're playing today."

"Don't give up on me," Cammy responded.

In the booth, Ted and I erased his name from the lineup card, but for some reason, Bochy did not.

Five minutes before game time, Caminiti appeared on the field. He stretched a little, made a few throws, and took a bite out of a Snickers candy bar. Remarkably, this man started the game at third base and batted cleanup. During the top of the second, he made a good play on a grounder hit by the Mets' Ray Ordonez. In his first plate appearance, Cammy homered over the center-field fence. His second at-bat, he belted a three-run homer to right center. A few innings later, he left the game and retired to the training table with another IV in his arm. After Caminiti went to the clubhouse, Wally Joyner immediately laid down on the dugout floor and asked for an IV and a Snickers bar. Is there any doubt about why teammates (and broadcasters) revered Ken Caminiti?

Playing in Pain

Unfortunately, Caminiti cannot be discussed without addressing his admitted steroid abuse. Ken Caminiti eventually died of a drug overdose on October 10, 2004. In 1996, I honestly did not know he was using steroids. It was not a hot-button topic of conversation in major league baseball at that time. I know he was a heavy user of creatine, which is legal. Knowing Cammy's mind-set, if the instructions on creatine said to use it twice a week, he might use it four times a week, figuring more is better. I do know he played the entire season with an extremely painful shoulder injury.

I wondered if Tony Gwynn suspected Caminiti of steroid use?

"Absolutely not," Tony replied. "In fact when we first traded for him, he came to my house for a long talk. He told me he used to use drugs, but not anymore. I told him if he followed hitting coach Merv Rettenmund's advice, he would at least double his home run output. I could see he had barely tapped his potential. It was just his mechanics were all screwed up. Merv did straighten out his mechanics, and I

Ken Caminiti became a legend when the Padres played the New York Mets in Monterrey, Mexico in 1996. From the San Diego Hall of Champions Collection

watched him working hard in the weight room and with extra batting practice. It never occured to me he might be on steroids."

In San Diego, Caminiti's locker was located just in front of the training room. Many times, I saw players head for the training room, look at Caminiti and decide maybe they didn't need treatment after all. The players knew the pain he endured. His daily commitment to remain in the lineup was an inspiration to everyone.

However, in a 2002 article in *Sports Illustrated*, Caminiti acknowledged the shoulder problem caused him to purchase steroids from a pharmacy in Tijuana, Mexico. He admitted overuse during the remainder of the season.

Another time, Bochy did not have Caminiti's name written on the lineup card. Cammy went into Bruce's office and tried to talk his way back into the lineup. Bochy remained adamant because Caminiti was dishonest about his pain.

According to Bochy, Cammy said, "If you put me back in the lineup, I promise to lie to you less!"

The Padres returned to San Diego from Mexico, and Caminiti slugged a grand slam in the first inning as the Padres beat Montreal 7-3. Two days later, he launched two more homers, including a three-run blast in the first as the Padres won 7-2 over the Expos. Cammy's three hits and two RBIs helped beat the Phillies 7-1 on August 24. The next day he had two more hits, and an RBI in an 11-2 victory against Philadelphia. Caminiti's two home runs produced a 3-2 win over the Mets in New York on August 28. The following day, his single in the ninth drove home the deciding run in another 3-2 win. Fueled by Caminiti, the Padres went 18-10 in August and began the final month with a 76-61 record, a scant game ahead of the Dodgers.

Battle for the Playoffs

Caminiti remained hot in September with nine homers and 23 RBIs in 25 games. However, the Dodgers had also played well. San Diego headed up the freeway for the final weekend of the season trailing Los Angeles by two games with three games left to play.

The Dodgers needed only one win to clinch. The Padres needed a sweep to finish first. Montreal was also a factor. The Expos were battling the Padres and Dodgers for the National League's wild-card spot.

In Game 1, the Dodgers led San Diego 2-1 in the eighth inning when the amazing Ken Caminiti tied the score with a home run, his 40th of the season. In the 10th, Steve Finley singled and scored on Cammy's double to grab the lead. San Diego added two more runs to win 5-2 as Trevor Hoffman recorded his 40th save.

In Game 2, the score was tied 2-2 in the eighth inning when the Padres loaded the bases with two outs. The Padres' hitting machine, Tony Gwynn, delivered a clutch two-run single, which he later rated the biggest hit of his 14-year career. Hoffman struck out the side in the ninth inning to preserve the 4-2 victory. The Padres were tied with the Dodgers for first place.

Over the years, the wild-card concept has been very successful in keeping teams in the playoff hunt that would otherwise be playing out the string. However, there is one major flaw, and it occurred in this series. The Padres' win on September 28 not only tied the Dodgers, but clinched a playoff berth for both teams because Montreal was eliminated with a loss. That meant the final game of the season, Sunday, September 29, would determine the winner of the National League West, but the loser would still be in the playoffs.

Obviously, much of the pressure was off both clubs.

His Finest Moment

The final game featured outstanding pitching. Bob Tewksbury started for San Diego and blanked the Dodgers on three hits through seven innings. Ramon Martinez, the Dodgers starter, only pitched one inning. Pedro Astacio followed Martinez and shut out the Padres into the eighth inning. Both bullpens continued to hang goose eggs until the 11th inning, when Finley and Caminiti led off with singles.

In his finest moment, Chris Gwynn delivered a pinch-hit two-run double for the only runs of the game.

"Watching Chris get that hit was one of the highlights of my life," Tony told me. "He'd obviously had a tough year, but it was his hit that sent us to the playoffs as Division champions."

Hoffman sat the Dodgers down in the ninth for his third save of the series. The NL West Champion Padres won 2-0. It was one of the greatest weekends in Padres history.

The Padres' final won-loss record was 91-71, second best in club history. The 1984 World Series team went 92-70, capping a remarkable comeback by the franchise.

Cardinals Sweep

Although all three games would be competitive, the St. Louis Cardinals swept the Padres.

The series began at Busch Stadium. Gary Gaetti hit a three-run homer in the first inning, which held up for a 3-1 Cardinals victory.

The Padres had opportunities, but stranded 10 men, including two in the ninth when Tony Gwynn's hot shot up the middle was snagged by relief ace Dennis Eckersley. It was the first of three saves for Eck in the abbreviated series.

In game two, the Padres tied the score 4-4 in the top of the eighth inning, only to have St. Louis score without a hit in the bottom of the frame for a 5-4 victory.

Action moved to San Diego for game three. Ken Caminiti's second home run of the series helped the Padres take a 4-1 lead into the sixth inning. However, the Cards tied the score with three in the sixth and forged a 5-4 lead with another run in the seventh. An inning later, the amazing Caminiti tied the score with yet another homer. It appeared the Padres would reclaim the lead when Jody Reed laced a bullet to right field with two outs and a runner on second. Brian Jordan made a miraculous diving catch to preserve the 5-5 tie. In the top of the ninth, Jordan belted a two-run homer off Trevor Hoffman. The Cardinals won 7-5 to complete the sweep.

Despite being down over the tough loss, loyal fans stayed in their seats to cheer the Padres. The players responded by returning to the field and applauding the fans. Even the St. Louis players and their contingent of wives and friends stopped their celebration on the field long enough to applaud the effort by the Padres.

The Year of Ken Caminiti

The Padres received many postseason honors. Tony Gwynn won his seventh silver bat with a .353 average. It was his third batting title in a row. Trevor Hoffman was named the NL Fireman of the Year with 42 saves—including 18 straight to end the season. Bruce Bochy was chosen as the NL Manager of the Year. Steve Finley received a Gold Glove and played in all but one game, batting .298 with 45 doubles, nine triples, 30 homers, 95 RBIs, and 22 stolen bases. He finished fifth in voting for Most Valuable Player and would have certainly received more MVP recognition if it weren't for Caminiti's remarkable season. There is no doubt this was the year of Ken Caminiti.

In addition to being the National League's unanimous choice as MVP, the hardnosed third baseman also won a Gold Glove. Cammy's bat produced a .326 average, 40 homers, and 130 RBIs.

He seemed good for at least one eye-popping defensive play in every game. In Miami on April 22, Greg Colbrunn of the Marlins hit a shot down the line. Caminiti backhanded the ball with a dive to his right and from a seated position, fired a laser to first to retire Colbrunn . . . the defensive play of the year in major league baseball.

Chapter 12

The Best Season—1998

Important Acquisitions

The 1998 season was easily the best in Padres history. The only blemish on a nearly perfect memory was the four-game sweep by the very talented and balanced New York Yankees in the World Series. A rather large blemish to be sure, but not one that ruined the accomplishments of this remarkable season.

Kevin Brown Acquired in a Fire Sale

Kevin Brown was acquired from the 1997 World Champion Florida Marlins in a deal that sent young first base prospect Derrek Lee to Florida. Marlins owner Wayne Huizenga had assembled an outstanding, but expensive Florida team for 1997. The Marlins were the NL wild-card team and reached the World Series with playoff wins over San Francisco and Atlanta. After Florida beat Cleveland in a seven-game World Series, Huizenga decided the cost of victory was too much. He claimed the Marlins still lost money and conducted a fire sale to get rid of high-priced players. The Padres had a veteran team with a small window of opportunity to win, so they rolled the dice. Derrek Lee was a number-one draft choice and considered a future star by San Diego baseball people. He proved they were right by developing into an All-Star first baseman and batting champion. However, Kevin Brown was a legitimate number-one starter and proved it with a terrific 1998 season.

Dave Stewart Became the Pitching Coach

In a subtle move, Kevin Towers convinced Dave Stewart to become the pitching coach. Stewart had worked as Towers's special assistant in 1997, but Kevin felt Stewart's intensity and pitching philosophy would have a major impact on the pitching staff. Stewart had been an outstanding major league pitcher, winning 20 games four times during a 15-year career. Known for his menacing glare while on the mound, he had been a member of three World Series championship teams. Stew wanted his starters to go deep into games to make the bullpen more effective. Admittedly, it's easier to be a good pitching coach when Kevin Brown leads your staff. However, Andy Ashby had his finest season as the number-two starter behind Brown, and all the other starters seemed to pitch longer. Trevor Hoffman, a great relief pitcher under any circumstances, enjoyed his best year in 1998 with 53 saves in 54 chances. Even in spring training, everyone sensed this could be a special team.

The night before the opening game in Cincinnati, I joined several fellow broadcasters for dinner at a well-known steak house. As we entered the restaurant, we spotted a group of about 15 people in a side room having a good time. The entire Padres pitching staff and catchers gathered for a season-opening bonding session.

Opening Day

The season opened March 31 at Riverfront Stadium with a Padres starting lineup that stayed intact for the whole year:

2B	Quilvio Veras
CF	Steve Finley
RF	Tony Gwynn
3B	Ken Caminiti
LF	Greg Vaughn
1B	Wally Joyner
C	Carlos Hernandez
SS	Chris Gomez

Kevin Brown started and proved as good as advertised. Brownie had a two-hit shutout going into the seventh inning. He also contributed a three-run double as the Padres breezed to a 10-2 win. Both

Wally Joyner and Tony Gwynn homered—for Gwynn, his first-ever opening-day home run. The magic had started. The Padres began the season 11-2 and finished April with a 19-7 mark and a five-game lead in the Western Division.

Greg Vaughn Plays Long Ball

In May, a series of injuries sidelined Gwynn, Joyner, Veras and Caminiti. The Padres went 16-14, but maintained a two-and-a-half-game lead in their division. The power of Greg Vaughn and relief work of Trevor Hoffman kept the Padres afloat. Vaughn unloaded 12 homers with 32 RBIs in 30 games while Hoffy registered eight saves with a 0.84 ERA. Healthier in June, the Padres responded with an 18-9 record that included an 11-game winning streak.

Vaughn's power surge continued with 10 homers and 24 RBIs, while Kevin Brown and Andy Ashby each won four games. After the Padres acquired catcher Jim Leyritz from the Boston Red Sox in June, he had an immediate impact, hitting a pair of doubles and three RBIs in a 5-3 win at Seattle. He would make significant contributions during the post season. The Padres' division lead increased to five and a half games.

Kevin Brown Plays Traffic Cop

In early July, the Padres were playing an inter-league game at Oakland when I witnessed an amazing display of leadership by Kevin Brown. The A's had scheduled a major promotion with fireworks and a crowd of over 40,000 gathered at the Oakland Coliseum. The Padres feared traffic would be a problem getting to our plane, and it was. The Padre busses were frozen in parking lot gridlock. Kevin Brown popped out of the players bus, stopped traffic, rerouted cars and cleared a path for the busses. Within 20 minutes, we were on our way to the airport. In 30 years of travel with the Padres, I have never seen anything like it. Brownie was our hero.

"Hells Bells"

On July 25, 1998, a tradition began that continues to thrill crowds at Petco Park. When Trevor Hoffman entered the game with

"Hells Bells" signals "Trevor Time" when Trevor Hoffman slams the door.
From the San Diego Hall of Champions Collection

a save on the line, the sound system blared the song, "Hells Bells," by AC/DC. The Qualcomm fans were blown away. Who came up with the idea of Trevor's musical accompaniment? It was a Padres salesman named Chip Bowers. Chip is gone from the organization, but his contribution will be remembered always.

That night, Hoffy preserved a 6-5 win over the Houston Astros by striking out Moises Alou to end the game. It was Trevor's 41st consecutive save, which at the time tied the major league record. Ironically, the following night, an Alou home run ended Hoffman's amazing streak. It was his only blown save of the season—regardless, the Padres ended up winning the game 5-4 in 10 innings.

To this day, Trevor will tell you that "Hells Bells" provides inspiration as he runs in from the bullpen.

In Hoffy's words, "The adrenaline starts to flow with the anticipation of the bells." Hoffman's "Hells Bells" introduction remains the coolest and the hottest in all of baseball.

The Long Hot Summer

July was another terrific month for San Diego. The team went 18-8 (71-38 overall) and led San Francisco by 13 games. Hoffman registered 11 saves with a 0.73 ERA in July. Vaughn swatted 11 more homers with 23 RBIs, and on July 12, Ken Caminiti homered three times to knock off Los Angeles 6-3. With another 18-victory month in August, the Padres made a shambles of the NL West race. Their record improved to 89-49, and their lead increased to 15 games over the Giants and 21 over the Dodgers. Vaughn added seven more homers and 16 RBIs. Caminiti powered eight homers and 18 RBIs. Hoffman contributed nine more saves, and Kevin Brown no-hit the Brewers for six and two-thirds innings before settling for a one-hit shutout 4-0.

The Padres made two personnel moves in August to prepare for the postseason. One worked; one didn't. Pinch-hitter deluxe John Vander Wal came from the Rockies and provided several key hits in the playoffs. Left-handed reliever Randy Myers was acquired from Toronto in one of the worst decisions in Padre history. San Diego wanted a left-handed relief pitcher for postseason play and desired to prevent Atlanta from picking up Myers. It turned out the Braves had no interest in the power pitcher, who had once been one of the best closers in the game. He helped the 1990 Reds win the World Series as a member of the famous "Nasty Boys" with Rob Dibble and Norm Charlton. Since then, he saved 38 games for the '92 Padres, 53 for the '93 Cubs, 45 for the '97 Baltimore Orioles and had 28 saves in Toronto when the Padres got him in a trade. They planned to rent Myers and his high salary for the stretch and postseason and then dump him. Unfortunately, his trademark fastball had been destroyed by a rotator-cuff injury. He never pitched for San Diego again, and his huge salary hung over the Padres budget like an albatross.

Clinching the Division in Dramatic Style

Local fans, unaccustomed to a cakewalk, watched the team stagger to the finish line with a 9-14 record in September. The team highlight occurred on September 12 when a crowd of 60,823 showed up in hopes the Padres would clinch the division that night against the Dodgers. Los Angeles led 7-0 going into the Padres fifth. A home run by Wally Joyner and two-run double by Chris Gomez made it a 7-3 game heading into the sixth inning.

In the sixth, with the crowd going nuts, the Padres sent 10 batters to the plate and scored five runs. Dodger pitching issued six walks and hit a batter. Greg Vaughn singled to start the uprising, and his second single drove home the fifth and winning run. Hoffman snuffed a Los Angeles rally in the ninth for his 49th save. The Padres clinched the division with a dramatic come-from-behind 8-7 victory.

Vaughn Hits 50 Home Runs

This was the year both Mark McGwire and Sammy Sosa broke Roger Maris's single-season home run record (61) with 70 and 66 homers respectively. To a lesser degree, but still impressive were Greg Vaughn's 50 homers. The muscular outfielder recorded his 49th home run of the season on September 14 and appeared a lock to become the first Padre to hit 50 homers in a season. Perhaps pressing too hard, Vaughn failed to reach that plateau in his next 40 plate appearances. Finally, in his last at-bat of the season, Greg homered to lead the Padres to a 3-2 triumph in Phoenix. What a season for Greg Vaughn! He finished the year batting .272 with 112 runs scored, 28 doubles, four triples, 50 home runs, and 119 RBIs. He also walked 79 times, stole 11 bases, and played in all but four games.

What a difference a year makes. . . .

In 1997, Vaughn batted .216 with 18 homers and 57 RBIs. The Padres made a deal to trade him to the Yankees for left-handed pitcher Kenny Rogers. Fortunately, Vaughn failed to pass the Yankees' physical exam and remained in San Diego. After 1998, the Padres were thankful the Yankee trade fell through. The team's final record was 98-64, the best ever.

Greg Vaughn hit 50 home runs for the 1998 National League champion Padres.
From the San Diego Hall of Champions Collection

Hoffy Should Have Won The Cy Young

When the regular season concludes, members of the Baseball Writers Association of America vote for the top individual awards. Two writers in each major league city have a vote on MVP, Cy Young Award, Rookie of the Year and Manager of the Year. Almost all the writers I have known over the years are very conscientious in their voting, and I rarely disagreed with their picks. Things were different in 1998. The 32 National League writers voting for the Cy Young winner chose Tommy Glavine. Glavine, a certain Hall of Famer, registered 20-6 with a 2.47 ERA in 1998. An excellent year—but in my view, Glavine fell short of the extraordinary season played by Trevor Hoffman.

Hoffman arguably had the greatest season ever for a relief pitcher in 1998. He appeared in 66 games with a record of 4-2 and 53 saves in 54 chances. In 73 innings, he allowed only 41 hits and 21 walks. Counting one hit batsman, Hoffy's opponents put just 63 runners on base in his 73 innings. Trevor gave up two homers and struck out 86 batters. Certainly, there was precedence for awarding the Cy Young to a relief pitcher. The Padres' Mark Davis won the award in 1989 with 44 saves, and Willie Hernandez of Detroit had 36 saves in 1984 when he received the honor in the American League.

Hoffman was clearly surprised. He politely inquired about the reasons the writers did not include him in their vote. All said, it was because, philosophically, they did not believe a relief pitcher should win the award. It was unfair. Hoffman picked the wrong year and the wrong group of voters for his magnificent season.

Houston, You Have a Problem

The playoffs began for the Padres at the Houston Astrodome. Houston had an outstanding team in 1998, serious World Series contenders. The Astros won 102 games and augmented an already impressive pitching staff with a big lefthander named Randy Johnson. The Big Unit went 10-1 with a 1.28 ERA after moving to Texas in mid-season and was especially tough in the Dome. The Padres countered with Kevin Brown, 18-7 with a 2.38 ERA. A pitching duel was expected, and it was delivered.

The game remained scoreless until Tony Gwynn led off the Padres sixth with a double and eventually scored on a Jim Leyritz sacrifice fly. Greg Vaughn made it 2-0 for San Diego with a home run in the eighth inning. Brown was magnificent. He struck out 16 and blanked the Astros on two hits through eight innings. Trevor Hoffman allowed an unearned run in the ninth, and the Padres captured Game 1, 2-1.

"Brown was electric that night, still throwing 97 miles per hour in the eighth inning," Tony Gwynn said. "Nobody was going to hit him."

Bruce Bochy had a deeper feeling. "Brownie's performance lifted the whole ball club, giving us a sense of confidence that we could beat the Astros."

Even at One Game Apiece

The second game matched a pair of pitchers coming off career years—Andy Ashby (17-9, 3.34) for San Diego and Shane Reynolds (19-8, 3.51) for the Astros. Ashby suffered an off day and left after four with Houston on top 3-0. RBI hits by Steve Finley and Gwynn made it a 3-2 game until Derek Bell homered for the Astros in the eighth. Trailing 4-2 and down to their last out in the ninth, Jim Leyritz sent a Billy Wagner fastball over the right field wall to tie the game at 4-4. The resilient Astros battled back in the bottom of the ninth, and Bill Spiers singled home the winning run.

The Playoffs Move to San Diego

Game 3 was played at Qualcomm Stadium before a roaring crowd of 65,235. Because of staggered days off to accommodate network television, Kevin Brown was able to start again with Mike Hampton on the mound for Houston. Another pitching duel ensued, with San Diego scoring first in the sixth inning. The Astros chased Brown and tied the score in the seventh. Amazing Jim Leyritz untied the score with a home run in the bottom of the inning.

The supremely self-confident Leyritz had been derisively labeled "The King" while he was with the New York Yankees. The nickname certainly fit his playoff heroics, and there were more to come. Protecting a 2-1 lead, Hoffman struck out the side in the ninth. The Padres were up two games to one.

Beating Randy Johnson for the Second Time

In the fourth game, the Padres again faced Randy Johnson. Sterling Hitchcock (9-7, 3.93) got the call for San Diego. An early Leyritz home run put the Padres on top in the second inning, but the Astros tied the score 1-1 in the fourth. The Padres got a huge break in the sixth inning, scoring the go-ahead run on a throwing error by Houston third baseman Sean Berry. Trailing 2-1 with the bases loaded in the seventh, the Astros were forced to pinch hit for Randy Johnson. Dan Miceli came out of the bullpen to get pinch-hitter Carl Everett on a pop up. In the eighth inning, the Padres put the game away on a two-run pinch double by John Vander Wal and a two-run homer by Wally Joyner. The Padres had defeated Randy Johnson twice in four games and captured the division series with a 6-1 victory in Game 4.

Bring Out the Brooms

The National League Championship Series began three days later, with the Padres facing another typically powerful Braves team in

Atlanta. The opening game matched Andy Ashby and John Smoltz. Both pitchers were on their game. An Andruw Jones homer was the only run Ashby allowed through seven innings. Sporting a .452 lifetime batting average against Smoltz, Tony Gwynn tied the score with a single in the fifth. Even on a ground out, Jim Leyritz drove in the go-ahead run in the eighth until an Andruw Jones sacrifice fly tied the score at two in the ninth. In the top of the 10th, Ken Caminiti homered over the center-field fence, and the Padres held on for a 3-2 extra-inning victory.

Kevin Brown was the story of Game 2. He pitched a complete-game three-hit shutout with 11 strikeouts. The final out was a strikeout of Braves left fielder Ryan Klesko. A two-out single by Quilvio Veras drove in the only run the Padres would need against Tommy Glavine. RBI singles by Steve Finley and Wally Joyner in the ninth made the final score 3-0 Padres. San Diego won the first two games of the series in Atlanta, and the next three games were scheduled for Qualcomm Stadium.

Sterling Hitchcock would face Greg Maddux. Maddux, a probable first-ballot Hall of Famer, was 18-9 with a 2.22 ERA in 1998. The game may have been decided by a defensive play in the third inning. The Braves had one run and Walt Weiss on second base with two outs. Chipper Jones laced a single to left, and John Vander Wal made a perfect throw to the plate. Leyritz did an outstanding job of blocking off Weiss, and the inning was over. The Braves did not score again, as Hitchcock—and the bullpen of Donne Wall, Dan Miceli, Randy Myers, and Trevor Hoffman—shut down the Atlanta attack. Meanwhile, the Padres got RBI hits from Steve Finley and Ken Caminiti in the fifth and added two more runs in the eighth with a Leyritz double being the key blow. The Padres had a 4-1 victory and, incredibly, a three-games-to-none lead in the playoff series.

Put Away the Brooms

The Padres were dreaming of a four-game sweep as they played the Braves in a late afternoon game on Sunday, October 11. Another home run by Leyritz and six solid innings on the mound by Joey Hamilton gave San Diego a 3-2 lead heading into the seventh inning. The Braves finally came to life. They exploded for six runs with the big blow—a grand slam by Andres Galarraga. With an 8-3 victory, Atlanta remained alive for Game 5.

The Padres were hoping for victory to avoid another trip back to Atlanta. Andy Ashby pitched six good innings for San Diego, allowing the Braves two runs. Ken Caminiti's two-run homer in the first and John Vander Wal's two-run homer in the sixth gave the Padres a 4-2 lead heading into the seventh inning. Padres Skipper Bruce Bochy rolled the dice and brought in his ace Kevin Brown to pitch in relief. The Braves had hardly touched Brown four days earlier, and the move looked brilliant as Brownie mowed down the Atlanta batters in the seventh.

Then came the eighth inning. A walk and an infield single brought Michael Tucker to the plate with one out. During the season, Brown had given up just three homers to left-handed hitters in 490 at-bats.

Tucker hit number four, a three-run bullet over the right-field wall, and the Braves grabbed a 5-4 lead.

"That homer was like a kick to the stomach," Bochy said. "In retrospect, I probably left Brownie in one hitter too long. Tucker had had some success against Kevin in the past, while Trevor Hoffman had good numbers with Tucker."

Atlanta scored two more runs off the Padres bullpen for a five-run inning and a 7-4 lead heading into the bottom of the ninth. Greg Myers quickly belted a two-run pinch homer for the Padres to make it a 7-6 game. Braves manager Bobby Cox summoned Greg Maddux in relief. Maddux had started just two days earlier and took the 4-1 loss. Tony Gwynn had a lifetime .400-plus batting average against Maddux. This time with the tying run on base, Maddux retired Tony on a sharp ground ball to first.

The Braves won 7-6, and the series was heading back to Georgia with the stunned Padres holding a three-games-to-two lead.

In Bochy's opinion: "I gave a lot of credit to Trevor Hoffman for keeping the team loose on the flight to Atlanta after that tough loss."

Break Out the Champagne

Sterling Hitchcock was set to start Game 6 for the Padres against the Braves' Tom Glavine. If a seventh game were necessary, Kevin

Brown would be the Padres' starter. Hitchcock and Glavine shut out both offenses for five innings. In the sixth, Greg Vaughn and Ken Caminiti singled, putting runners on first and third. Jim Leyritz' ground out scored Vaughn and advanced Caminiti to second. Wally Joyner followed with an RBI single to center: 2-0 Padres. Steve Finley singled, Chris Gomez walked, and Hitchcock hit a flare to left field that was muffed by Danny Bautista. Two more runs came across to make it 4-0 Padres. Quilvio Veras followed with another run-scoring single, and the San Diego lead grew to 5-0. That's the way the game ended. Trevor Hoffman wrapped things up 1-2-3 in the ninth. The Padres were going to the World Series for a second time. How about Sterling Hitchcock? He started and won three playoff games, defeating three Cy Young Award winners—all probable Hall of Famers: Randy Johnson, Greg Maddux, and Tommy Glavine.

Her Cap Was Set on Fire

The day before the World Series opened in New York, I was awakened in my hotel room by an early morning phone call. It was my youngest daughter, Jill, currently an assignment editor for KUSI-TV News in San Diego. Jill had hitched a flight with one of her roommates, who was an airline stewardess. They flew all night and invited me to join their group for breakfast at an Irish pub near the hotel. Her arrival was a total surprise, but I was able to locate some World Series tickets, and they were featured on national television wearing large sombreros while swaying back and forth in the upper deck during the Yankees' Game 2 victory. After the game, she showed more courage than sense by entering a bar near Yankee Stadium wearing a Padres cap. Soon her cap was set on fire. Fortunately, it was no longer on her head. She and her group handled the situation so well that within a few minutes, the Yankees fans were lining up to buy these crazy Californians some beers.

Raising daughters is not a simple task.

It Was Strike Three!

The Series opened Saturday, October 17, in the House that Ruth Built. Kevin Brown started for the Padres and San Diegan David Wells was the Yankees' man. In the second inning, Ricky Ledee's two-run double put the Yankees up 2-0, but Greg Vaughn followed with a two-run homer of his own to tie the score in the third. Two innings later, Tony Gwynn and Vaughn hit back-to-back home runs, and the Padres grabbed a 5-2 lead. Brown seemed to have New York in check until a case of the flu finally caught up and forced him from the game in the seventh. The Yankees quickly tied the game on Chuck Knoblauch's three-run homer off reliever Donne Wall. The Bombers then loaded the bases with two out. The Padres brought in southpaw Mark Langston to face left-handed-hitting Yankees first baseman Tino Martinez. The Padres felt Langston struck Martinez out with a 2-2 fastball, which should have ended the inning. Richie Garcia, the home plate umpire, saw it differently, and the count was full.

"To this day I still see that pitch in my mind," said Bochy. "I thought there was no doubt it was strike three."

Langston's next pitch landed in the right-field bleachers for a grand slam. The blow powered the Yankees to a 9-6 victory. The Padres and their fans were left to wonder what might have happened if Kevin Brown had been able to stay in the game. If Langston's pitch had been called strike three, the game would have gone to the eighth tied at five. Replays of the controversial pitch indicated it was a strike, but to hang the outcome of the game on a single pitch is folly. Hundreds of close calls are made in every game. Some go your way, some go the other way.

Still. . . .

Yankees Take Game 2

The second game belonged completely to the Yankees. Right fielder Paul O'Neill made a spectacular catch to rob Wally Joyner of a three-run homer in the opening inning. In the bottom stanza, Ken Caminiti committed an error that kept the inning alive and allowed the Yankees to score three times. Those two plays resulted in a six-run swing. Padres starter Andy Ashby gave up seven runs in less than three innings. The Yankees had 16 hits including homers by Bernie Williams and Jorge Posada and breezed to a 9-3 win in the Big Apple.

The Series Shifted to Qualcomm

The series shifted to Qualcomm Stadium for Game 3—a must-win situation for the Padres to stay in the hunt. Sterling Hitchcock took the mound against David Cone, a 20-game winner for the Yankees. The brilliant Hitchcock shut out the Yankees for six innings and triggered a three-run Padre rally in the bottom of the sixth with a leadoff single. Gwynn and Caminiti drove in two of the runs with the third coming home on an error. The Yankees came back with two runs in the seventh, one on a homer by third baseman Scott Brosius. They might have scored more but for a great catch by shortstop Chris Gomez on a line drive by Derek Jeter with two runners on board. Gomez turned the catch into an inning-ending double play. It was 3-2 Padres when Randy Myers faced left-handed Paul O'Neill, who worked a base on balls.

"Hell's Bells" blared over Mission Valley as Trevor Hoffman entered the game—one of the loudest ovations I have ever heard. Trevor retired Bernie Williams but walked Tino Martinez. Scott Brosius was the batter. Brosius had his best season in 1998, batting .300 with 19 homers and a career-high 98 RBIs. Hoffman had struck him out at the All-Star Game. This time, Brosius belted a 424-foot home run over the center-field fence to give the Yankees a 5-3 lead. The Padres added a run in the eighth to make it 5-4. Yankees relief ace Mariano Rivera had retired two in the ninth when pinch hitters Carlos Hernandez and Mark Sweeney both singled. Rivera struck out Andy Sheets, though, and the Yankees took a commanding 3-0 lead in the Series.

The King Ran Out of Miracles

Kevin Brown was San Diego's last chance in Game 4 against New York's Andy Pettitte. Brown held the Yankees scoreless through six innings, but the Yankees got on the board in the seventh and added two in the eighth for a 3-0 lead.

Pettitte tired in the eighth. The Padres loaded the bases with two outs, and Leyritz came to bat. Against his old teammates, "The King" ran out of miracles. Rivera retired him on a line drive to center. The Yankees completed a four-game sweep with a 3-0 victory before a record crowd of 65,427 at Qualcomm.

The Most Awe-Inspiring Love-In
this Side of Woodstock

What happened after the game?

Here's what columnist Lisa Olson wrote in the New York *Daily News:*

"The baseball season ended as it should have, with one of the most awe-inspiring love-ins this side of Woodstock. If you weren't moved by what happened in San Diego after the Yankees won the World Series on Wednesday night, then you've been sniffing too many oily mitts, because baseball has never experienced anything like it. The Padres were swept out of the Series, then swept away by an outpouring of raw emotion that surely had enough power to cure America's cynical soul. While the Yankees were in the visitors clubhouse, getting doused by champagne, the Padres were being showered with kisses and tears and unconditional love. Twenty minutes after the final out, the Padres were being serenaded back onto the field, the fans clapping until their palms were raw. Encores rarely are meant for losers, but 65,427 folks, the largest baseball crowd in the city's history, simply refused to leave, waving their white rally towels, not in surrender, but in jubilation."

Two days later, the team was honored by a parade that passed thousands lining the streets of downtown San Diego. Riding in open cars, manager Bruce Bochy, players, coaches, and front-office executives waved as the love-in continued. Two weeks later, the citizens of San Diego voted overwhelmingly to help finance a new downtown ballpark, which took two extra years to manifest because of 17 lawsuits filed by people who apparently didn't believe in a democratic vote. All 17 lawsuits were eventually dismissed, and Petco Park, the new home of the Padres, opened in 2004.

Chapter 13

Potpourri

Damn Lights!

The major league Padres began play at San Diego Stadium in 1969. Their final season at the stadium was 2003. In 35 years of play, whether it was San Diego Stadium, Jack Murphy Stadium, or Qualcomm Stadium, the lights were a problem for the third baseman and the left fielder. The major leaguers actually had a preview of what was to come in 1968, when the Pacific Coast League Padres played their final season in the stadium. Their home opener was a night game. The first play of the game was a groundball to third. Johnny Werhas lost the ball in the lights.

First Game

The first official major league game at San Diego Stadium was April 8, 1969. A crowd of only 23,370 showed up to watch this historic contest, and the fans were treated to an excellent pitchers duel. Dick Selma hurled the Padres to a 2-1 victory over Houston with a complete-game five-hitter and 12 strikeouts. When Selma beat Astros ace Don Wilson, he had some extra incentive. The night before at the Baseball Writers preseason dinner, Wilson had told the Padres starter that there was no way he would win. Selma won only one more game for the Padres before being traded to the Chicago Cubs for pitchers Joe Niekro and Gary Ross and infielder Francisco Libran.

The Padres' first opening-day lineup looked like this:

SS	Rafael Robles
2B	Roberto Pena
CF	Tony Gonzalez
RF	Ollie Brown
1B	Bill Davis
LF	Larry Stahl
3B	Ed Spiezio
C	Chris Cannizzaro
P	Dick Selma

Cannizzaro's main memory of the game was catching a winner. "I loved to catch a winning game. Selma had a dominating curve that night and a sailing fastball that he could also cut."

The first Padres hit was a home run by Ed Spiezio in the fifth inning. He is also credited with scoring and driving in the first run. The winning run scored on an RBI double by Ollie Brown in the sixth inning. The Padres had just four hits in the game—Selma had two of them.

Padres president Buzzie Bavasi called the game "The most gratifying night of my career."

Baseball in the Snow

Major league baseball used to showcase the opening game of each season in Cincinnati in tribute to the 1869 Red Stockings, baseball's first professional team. In 1977, the Padres had the honor of visiting Cincinnati for the April 6 opener.

I remember waking up that morning anxious for the season to begin. I opened the blinds of my hotel room to see a blizzard outside. Eventually, two inches of snow would fall, and I figured there was very little chance of baseball that day.

I was wrong.

Batting practice was cancelled as was infield practice. Right up to the scheduled 2:30 p.m. start, snowplows were pushing snow against the stands. Game temperature was 38 degrees.

Gene Richards, batting leadoff for the Padres, hit a routine grounder to the Reds' Hall of Fame second baseman, Joe Morgan. It was so cold that the ball clanked off the glove of the usually sure-handed Reds infielder for an error. The 1977 championship season was underway.

The Reds had been World Series champions in 1975 and 1976 and won this game 5-3. Randy Jones took the loss and blamed himself for pitching mistakes. He dismissed the weather as a factor. But how could the weather not be a factor? There was a picture in the *Cincinnati Enquirer* newspaper the next morning of Padres utility man Bobby Valentine building a snowman in the dugout.

I don't know if it was the most unusual opening game I ever broadcast, but it definitely was the coldest.

What A Throw!

Which Padres outfielder had the best throwing arm? In my view, it's pretty close between the first pick in the 1968 expansion draft, Ollie Brown, and the best athlete in club history, Dave Winfield. However, there is no doubt about the throw that I remember most.

Jerry Turner was an outfielder with the Padres during the 1970s. He was a tough left-handed hitter who once beat the Cubs' great relief pitcher Bruce Sutter with a pair of two-run homers. One home run tied the game in the eighth inning, and the other won the game in the 10th.

Defense was another story. Jerry was playing left field at San Diego Stadium against St. Louis when the Cardinals loaded the bases. The next batter hit a clean single to left that Turner fielded on one hop and started to throw home. In mid-throw, he changed his mind and decided to throw to third base instead. In the process of changing his mechanics, Jerry threw across his body, and the ball flew down the left field line toward the San Diego bullpen. Fans were stunned to watch Turner run down his own throw in the bullpen as Redbirds flew around the bases.

Jerry later asked me how I had called the play on radio.

I didn't know what to say. . . .

Self-Preservation Comes First

Bill Greif, a good guy with a lively fastball, had a habit of throwing high and tight when he had an 0-2 count. In a 1975 game against Philadelphia, burly outfielder Greg Luzinski took exception to

Greif's chin music and charged the mound. A major fight ensued, and a reporter later asked Phillies relief ace Tug McGraw who he fought.

"I went immediately after Dan Frisella," replied Tug.

Why Frisella? He had nothing to do with the skirmish.

"He's renting my house in Poway," McGraw continued. "I wanted to make sure he didn't get hurt!"

A Tradition Begins

Major League Baseball's All-Star Game is now a two-day extravaganza with numerous activities scheduled the day before the game, including the popular home run derby. Hard to believe now, but there was a time when the National and American League All-Stars would work out and hold batting practice in an empty stadium the day before the game. The public was not permitted to watch.

San Diego had been awarded the All-Star Game for 1978, so the Padres director of business operations, Elten Schiller, traveled to New York's Yankee Stadium in 1977 to check out the procedures for conducting the game. Elten told me he rode the American League bus to the stadium where approximately 1,000 kids were waiting outside hoping to get a glimpse of their heroes. The bus drove past the youngsters, depositing the players at the stadium entrance, leaving a multitude of disappointed boys and girls outside.

The thought occurred to Schiller, "Why not let the kids in to see batting practice?"

In 1978, the Padres did just that. Parking was free, entrance to the stadium was free with seating on a first-come, first-serve basis, and the concession stands were open. Elten said he was hoping for a crowd of 15,000, which was the break-even point for Padres expenses. "Instead, over 30,000 showed up, and the event was a terrific success," recalled Schiller.

That night at a reception, Elten encountered Commissioner Bowie Kuhn, who questioned, "How come we didn't think of this before?"

Now it is an integral part of the game and has grown in stature. In 1992, when the Padres again hosted the All-Star game, I was on the field interviewing the all-stars over the public address system in front of 50,000 fans.

Everything began when Elten Schiller saw those disappointed youngsters standing outside Yankee Stadium in 1977.

Another interesting aspect to batting practice in 1978—"juiced" baseballs were served to the National League sluggers, who buried them deep in the bleachers while the American Leaguers watched on in admiration. When it was the Americans' turn to hit, regular baseballs were used. The NL power display probably had no effect on the game's outcome, but the Nationals did win 7-3.

Jackie Robinson Re-Visited

Ed Stevens was a longtime Padres scout who was added to the coaching staff in 1981 to qualify for the baseball pension. He was a courtly, southern gentleman from Galveston, Texas, with a pleasant drawl. One day, we were talking together on the team bus, and I asked him about his career. Stevens broke in with Brooklyn in 1945 and played in 99 games at first base for the Dodgers in 1946. He had 10 homers and 60 RBIs in 103 games. I remember reflecting, "Ed, you were there when Jackie Robinson broke the color line. Tell me about it."

Stevens's demeanor immediately changed, "It was the worst time of my life."

Although Jackie Robinson's primary position was second base, Dodgers owner Branch Rickey wanted him to start at first base, figuring that would ease his transition into the majors.

"Rickey told me he was sending me down to the minors on a temporary basis until Robinson got settled," Stevens said. "Then he would bring me back up to the Dodgers."

Robinson played 151 games at first base, was named NL Rookie of the Year, and helped Brooklyn win the 1947 pennant. Stevens was never recalled by Rickey and still bears scars from the situation.

Ed told me the abuse he took at home in the off-season was harsh. Knowing the attitude of the Deep South in the late 1940s, most of his friends couldn't understand how he lost his job to a black man.

Stevens did return to the major leagues in 1948 as a first baseman for Pittsburgh and led the league in fielding at .996. His last year in the majors was 1950.

How God Got His Nickname

In May of 1984, the Padres were at Shea Stadium for a three-game series against the New York Mets. The forecast was for rain and more rain. The umpire crew chief was Doug Harvey, who generally is considered to have been one of the all-time best umpires in the game. Harvey had an on-field reputation for no-nonsense, but off the field, he is a wonderful storyteller. It was during the first game of this soggy series in New York that Doug Harvey got his nickname.

It had rained heavily before the game started, and Mets general manager Frank Cashen wanted to get the contest in the books and the money in the bank. Harvey was behind home plate that evening and assured the anxious GM that he would do everything he could to start and finish the game. Doug took pride in the fact that his crew consistently had the fewest number of rainouts in the league. Ball clubs do not like to hand out rain checks, and umpires do not like to work doubleheaders.

In the second inning, the Mets took a 3-0 lead. Steve Garvey slipped in the mud while fielding a ground ball hit by Darryl Strawberry. According to Doug, Garvey had waved off the pitcher, Eric Show, indicating he would make the play unassisted. When the Garv slipped, Show was not on first to take the throw. Strawberry came around to score the Mets' first run, and New York added two more in the inning. The Padres got on the board with a run in the top of the third, but play was suspended the next inning because weather conditions made the field unplayable. There was a break in the action that lasted over an hour.

Harvey immediately headed to the umpires room to change into dry clothes, but his partner, Joe West, made a brief detour into the Padres dugout. By the time West got to the umpires room, his laughter was uncontrollable. He told his fellow umpires that Garvey had whined, "Dadgummit, Joe, didn't anybody think to check the infield before this game?"

West assured Garvey that "the chief" had inspected the field carefully before the game started. Terry Kennedy was taking off his catcher's gear at the other end of the dugout and heard the exchange. He slammed his shin guards down on the bench and bellowed, "Well, that doesn't matter—that son of a bitch walks on water!"

The remaining games in New York were rained out, and Harvey's crew moved on to Chicago. Jerome Holtzman of the *Chicago Tribune* heard about Kennedy's line and the surrounding circumstances, and he wrote a column for his paper with this headline: "God visits Chicago."

When asked to confirm the story, Terry Kennedy, who is now the manager of the San Diego Surf Dawgs in the Golden Baseball League, agreed.

"I meant to insult Harvey, but he loved it."

Incidentally, the Padres came back to win the game 5-4, and Terry was my guest on the postgame show. I didn't know then to ask him about his comment to Joe West. Likewise, Kennedy certainly didn't realize that Doug Harvey and Jerome Holtzman would find his flippant remark so entertaining.

And that is how God got his nickname.

Kevin Mitchell

I like Kevin Mitchell. He's a San Diego guy who survived a tough upbringing to become an outstanding major league player. In the 1986 World Series, he contributed a key pinch-hit in the ninth inning of Game 6 to help the Mets stage a dramatic comeback against the Boston Red Sox. Mitchell came to the Padres in a multiplayer deal that December. Kevin McReynolds was the key player in the trade for the Mets, while the rebuilding Padres received Mitchell along with young outfielders Stan Jefferson and Shawn Abner.

During spring training in Yuma, I did a pregame interview with Kevin. Numerous stories had appeared in the newspapers about Mitchell's past, including a number of physical altercations.

I asked him about the fights, and he replied, "Oh, Bob, I haven't been in a fight in a long time."

"How long?" I asked.

"Not since Christmas," replied Mitchell.

Kevin was set to play third base for the 1987 Padres. He informed the pitching staff not to worry about hitting batters while pitching inside. Mitchell assured the pitchers that, if any batter charged the mound, he would get to them first and take care of the situation.

The 1987 Padres got off to a miserable start. With one-third of the season gone, the team was on a pace to win just 36 games with a 12-42 record.

On the Fourth of July, the Padres and Giants got together on a seven-player deal. Kevin Mitchell and pitchers Dave Dravecky and Craig Lefferts went to San Francisco; Chris Brown and pitchers Mark Grant, Mark Davis, and Keith Comstock came to San Diego. The Giants really wanted Dravecky to help in their pennant run. The Padres coveted All-Star third baseman Chris Brown to replace Mitchell, who, in the opinion of the Padres braintrust, had too many "distractions" to play in San Diego.

Dravecky did help the Giants reach the playoffs, but eventually lost his left arm to cancer. Mitchell hit 15 home runs during the second half of the season and later was the 1989 National League's MVP with 47 homers and 125 RBIs.

Chris Brown was a bust for the Padres. He never seemed to recover from a beaning and was out of baseball by 1990.

Mark Davis developed into a terrific closer for San Diego. In 1989, the same year Mitchell was MVP, Davis saved 44 of 48 games to win the NL Cy Young Award.

Bogus No-Hitter

Every major league baseball game has someone assigned as an official scorer. For many years, a baseball writer covering the games performed the task. In the early 1980s, newspapers across the country decided it was a conflict of interest and prohibited their writers from official scoring. It was up to the home team to find as qualified a person as possible to do the job. The scorer is not an employee of the team but is paid by major league baseball to make scoring decisions during the game and file an official report following the contest.

I don't remember the name of the official scorer in Atlanta on September 11, 1991, but he made the most blatant hometown call that I have ever seen and I've seen a lot of them over the years.

The Padres still had an outside chance at the division title when they opened a two-game series against the Braves with Atlanta leading San Diego by seven and a half games. A sweep by the Padres was considered essential. The game turned into a terrific pitchers duel with the Braves winning 1-0. However, that's just part of the story.

Atlanta pitchers Kent Mercker (six innings), Mark Wohlers (two innings) and Alejandro Pena (one inning) were credited with the first-ever combined no-hitter in National League history. It should not have been allowed.

Two were out in the ninth inning when Padres centerfielder Darrin Jackson hit a high chopper to Braves third baseman Terry Pendleton. Pendleton lost the ball in the lights, turned his head and just stuck out his glove. The ball bounced off his glove, and the official scorer ruled the play an error to keep the no-hitter alive. Tony Gwynn flied out to left field, and the phony no-hitter was preserved.

Terry Pendleton had homered for the only run of the game and was my guest on the postgame show. Although he was pleased the error call kept the no-hitter going, Pendleton confirmed he could not see Jackson's chopper and just stuck his glove out.

In the Braves locker room after the game, I spotted the official scorer getting autographs on his scorecard from the three pitchers involved in the no-hitter.

What a professional. . . .

We're Number One!

Charles S. "Chub" Feeney had a long and distinguished career in major league baseball. He was essentially the general manager for the Giants, both in New York and San Francisco from 1946-1969. Feeney was the president of the National League from 1970-1986 and agreed to serve as Padres president in 1987. On September 24, 1988, Chub was watching the game from owner Joan Kroc's box on Fan Appreciation Night. The Padres were in the process of recording a 3-0 win over the Astros, which Ted Leitner and I were describing on cable TV.

Not all of the fans appreciated Feeney. Several were parading through the stands carrying a bed sheet that read, "Scrub Chub." One of our cable cameramen showed the sheet, then panned up to the owner's box where Chub suddenly gave the one-finger salute. Unfortunately for Chub, it was shown on live TV. In our booth,

When Padres president Chub Feeney flipped the bird, Ted Leitner (right) quipped, "Look Bob, I guess our president feels the fans are number one." From the Bob Chandler collection

Leitner said, "Look Bob, I guess our president feels the fans are number one."

Maureen O'Connor, the mayor of San Diego, was also enjoying the game from the owner's box. According to reports, she saw the incident and mentioned it to Mrs. Kroc, who confronted Feeney. He denied the event occurred.

On the 11:00 p.m. news that night, several television stations showed the gesture with footage from our cable telecast.

The next day, Chub Feeney resigned as Padres president.

Roseanne Barr

No one who heard Roseanne Barr sing the National Anthem at Qualcomm Stadium will ever forget it. The Padres were playing a doubleheader against Cincinnati on July 25, 1990. It was Working Women's day at the stadium, and Roseanne sang the anthem between games.

Let's set the scene:

Earlier in the 1990 season, Tom Werner and a group of 14 businessmen, mostly from San Diego, had purchased the Padres from

Joan Kroc. Werner was the chairman and managing partner. He was also a major television producer from Los Angeles. His production company had produced *The Cosby Show* and currently boasted the number-one rated TV show in the country, *Roseanne*.

Andy Strasberg was the Padres' director of marketing. He received a phone call from Werner who asked, "What do you think of Roseanne Barr singing the National Anthem?"

Andy thought it was a good idea, but replied, "Can she sing?"

"Makes no difference," said Werner. "Will the fans enjoy it?"

Strasberg felt they would, and plans were made for the big day.

To prevent any problems and avoid delays in the public address system, the Padres like to have singers record the anthem in advance. They lip synch their performance on camera. Andy recalled Werner turning down this request saying, "She won't do that, but it's not necessary because she's a pro."

The night before the event, Strasberg watched Roseanne sing "Kung Foo Fighting" on the *Tonight Show*. He became concerned. "She was awful," remembered Strasberg—but it was too late to do anything about it.

Roseanne talked with several players before her performance, and one of them asked her if she was going to grab herself and spit like the players. This was obviously on her mind as she approached the microphone to sing the anthem live.

Americans do not like singers to trifle with the National Anthem, and that sentiment is particularly strong in a military town like San Diego. Her lack of vocal talent became immediately obvious, and the fans began booing. Due to the public address system delays, she probably couldn't hear boos—so she stuck her fingers in her ears, drawing further contempt from the fans. When she tried to sing louder, the booing grew louder. Sure enough, Roseanne grabbed her crotch and spat on the ground when she finished. Ron Seaver, who was next to Roseanne and her husband, Tom Arnold, said Roseanne felt awful. She knew immediately her attempts at humor had failed badly. Seaver didn't know quite what to do. He asked the couple if they wanted to be escorted to their front-row seats? Arnold replied, "What, are you [bleeping] me? The fans are going to [bleeping] kill us."

Roseanne and Tom headed for their limo and fled the premises.

Up in the owner's box, Tom Werner quickly gathered his top executives along with Strasberg and Seaver. The second game of the doubleheader was beginning, but the media in attendance wanted to talk to Werner about the incident. They were banging on the door. Werner wanted no part of the media, and Seaver became the designated speaker. Ron told me, "It was the only time I ever talked to Werner during my tenure with the Padres."

To this day, Seaver is convinced Roseanne's intentions were good—that she just got caught up in something that spiraled out of control.

Roseanne's rendition of the anthem was played on morning radio across the country and remained a major story for several weeks. In fact, people in San Diego still talk about the incident.

Tom Werner is a good guy and is now one of the owners of the Boston Red Sox—and it's unlikely Roseanne will ever sing the National Anthem at Fenway Park.

Chapter 14

On the Road

Bump in the Road

Occasionally, on road trips, something unusual will happen. After a night game in Cincinnati, we all boarded one bus for the trip to our airplane, which was located in Kentucky. Normally, it's about a 30-minute ride, but our bus driver tried to take a short cut. We ended up lost on a dirt road near the airport.

Traveling secretary John "Doc" Mattei recalled ". . . hearing a metal crunching noise as the driver backed up. The bus had backed into a car in a secluded lover's lane."

About 40 players and staff looked out the windows as the couple in the car tried frantically to put their clothes back on. It was quite a show for the Padres traveling party as coach Whitey Wietelmann went outside to get the necessary accident paperwork completed. The poor girl was crying—she had borrowed the car for her evening date.

Imagine that explanation to an insurance agent. . . .

Prepared for Las Vegas

One night during spring training in the early 1980s, we prepared to check in at the Flamingo Hotel in Las Vegas for a weekend series of exhibition games. John Mattei pulled out his Padres credit card to get the room keys as the players were anxious to head for the gaming tables.

John "Doc" Mattei. From the Bill Swank Collection

The night clerk was unimpressed with a major league baseball team credit card and refused. "I can't give you the room keys because you have not yet established credit at the hotel."

Following an argument with the clerk, Mattei turned to pitcher John "The Count" Montefusco and jokingly said, "Count, pay him off."

Montefusco, obviously prepared for a night of gambling, calmly pulled out a huge roll of bills and pealed off $4,500 to pay for the first and last night's lodging. Mattei then wrote "The Count" a check for $4,500, which the casino clerk immediately cashed without first establishing credit.

Believe What I Say, Not What You See

In early June 1987, the Padres were trying to catch a late-night flight from Montreal to Atlanta. There was a strictly enforced 1:00 a.m. curfew for flights out of Dorval Airport. Canadian custom officials were doing their best to help the team through the procedure. As customs officers were waving us through the line, Kevin Mitchell dropped a clothes bag in front of an inspector. The inspector had no choice but to ask Mitchell to open the bag, which revealed two new $250 suits.

Duty was required, but Mitchell protested. "I bought these suits last year in Montreal, and I just brought them back for alterations."

Would you believe that story? Neither did the inspector—especially after he found a sales slip from the same day inside the bag. Mitchell still balked at paying duty, which caused a delay in the flight. Mattei went to manager Larry Bowa and told him, "If we blow this flight, I have to find hotel rooms to stay over in Montreal and fly to Atlanta tomorrow. I'm not doing that. If you want your third baseman on the airplane, you better intervene."

Bowa did intervene—the traveling secretary paid the duty, and the charter flight beat curfew by five minutes.

Jolly Rollie

Two busses are used now to transport the Padres. However, in the early days, we all traveled together on one bus. There was always great dialogue between the players and traveling secretary Doc Mattei.

Maybe you had to be there to fully appreciate the fun, but Hall of Fame relief pitcher Rollie Fingers and Mattei shared perhaps the most interesting exchanges.

Rollie hated to wait a full hour after a getaway game to take the bus to the airport. Finally, he decided to take a 12-passenger van instead. Once aboard the van, Fingers complained and complained about the slow speed until the driver had Rollie removed. One of baseball's best relief pitchers waited on the side of the road to flag down the team bus. You can just imagine the reception he received when he boarded the bus and explained his situation.

Another time, Fingers was on the bus complaining about his dead arm after pitching in three straight games. Doc Mattei hollered, "Rollie, why not leave your dead arm with all those other dead arms?" When the players spotted the passing cemetery, the bus exploded with laughter.

"He Tried to Get Up"

Gravel-voiced Doc Mattei loves to talk, and sometimes it gets him in trouble.

"I was taping a guy's ankle on the trainer's table and talking to another guy, doing it real fast. Somehow, the tape caught the corner of the table, and I kept going round and round. When he tried to get up, he was taped to the table."

Who Says Travel Is Not a Contact Sport?

Brian Prilaman began as a batboy with the Padres in 1971 and now serves the organization as director of team travel. 1998 was his first year in that capacity, and he will never forget his first trip to Montreal as travel director.

"The team plane landed at Mirabel Airport, which is a little farther out of town. It was late at night, and to make matters worse, the freeway was closed."

Naturally, the drivers of the two busses got lost in some residential area. "It was like *Ground Hog Day*," recalled Prilaman. "As we passed the same building four times!"

The players were frustrated and began to give the bus drivers and Prilaman a hard time.

"Finally, I snapped and got a little physical with the lead driver," laughed Prilaman. "I told him to get his butt in gear, call somebody, and get directions to the hotel."

It was now about four in the morning, and a young adult was walking up the street returning from work. Brian remembered, "One of the players left the bus and asked the kid if he knew how to get to the Sheraton Hotel? He did, and the players gave him some money, which probably came to about $1,000, to direct us. It took two turns and about five minutes, and we were there. Nice payday for less than 10 minutes effort. Later that night, we found out where he worked—a popular Montreal restaurant and bar called Winchell's Pub. When we spotted the kid, he was working as a busboy. This time the beers were on him."

Chapter 15

Characters

Dick Williams

Dick Williams was hired to manage the Padres in 1982 and inherited the same players who ended the strike-shortened 1981 season with a 41-69 record. Williams guided the team to identical 81-81 records in 1982 and 1983. In 1984, the Padres won their first National League pennant with a 92-70 finish.

Williams was a stickler for fundamentals. If you didn't perform them to his satisfaction, you simply didn't play. During games, he would stand at the end of the dugout and constantly write notes. He was interested in whether a player got a bunt down, advanced a runner to third with no outs, or drove in a runner from third with less than two outs.

Dick once stopped at my seat on the team airplane while I was recording the players' statistics. "You can take those numbers and shove them," he remarked, "I'm interested in the statistics that win games."

Some managers tell the team at the beginning of spring training to not worry about performance the first two weeks. Spend the time getting in shape, and then the manager would begin evaluations. Not Williams—he informed the players they would be judged starting with the first drill in the spring.

Tim Flannery remembered Williams's first comments to the team the opening day of spring training, 1982: "I don't care if you guys like me or not."

Many of the players did not like Williams, but in Flannery's opinion, "He was demanding, but he taught us how to play baseball, how to win."

Bunting for Dollars

I remember a simple bunting drill Dick devised to have some fun and also encourage the players to focus harder. He would spread paper money on the field as areas of emphasis for the bunting drills. For instance, $20 bills would be placed at the optimum spot to bunt, $10 bills at a good position, $5 dollar bills at an acceptable, but less desirable spot and $1 dollar bills at a borderline acceptable area. Each player could pick up the cash depending where his bunts went. It wasn't a lot of money, but it definitely improved the effort.

Dick's First Game

The Padres opened the 1982 season at San Diego Stadium on April 6 against the Atlanta Braves. In a terrific match up, Rick Mahler outdueled Juan Eichelberger, and the Braves won 1-0.

I was handling public relations for the Padres at the time and went to Dick's office after the game. Williams was fine dealing with the media, answering every question. Finally, there was one young reporter remaining in the office.

Apparently, the reporter intentionally waited for everyone to leave before asking, "Uh, Dick, in lieu of how the game turned out, are you now second-guessing yourself for not pinch-hitting for Eichelberger when the bases were loaded?"

Now that might seem like a reasonable question—except this situation happened in the second inning! Williams just stared at the guy until the reporter repeated, "Well, are you?"

Dick's jaw tightened, and he responded, "Don't ever ask me a question like that again."

I quickly escorted the guy out of Williams's office—I learned he had never covered a major league game and was representing a free, weekly paper. Somehow he slipped through the cracks and received a media pass for the game.

The Timid Texan

Dick's personality ranged from genial to sarcastic. I experienced both extremes. He also used the media to get a point across to one of his players. After one game, he was in his office with several reporters when he remarked that Waco native Andy Hawkins was the only "timid Texan" he had ever known.

Naturally, that quote appeared in the next morning's newspapers, and Hawkins was scheduled to pitch that night for the Padres.

Early in the afternoon, Hawkins stormed into the clubhouse and headed straight for the manager's office. He banged on the door. Later, loud noises could be heard inside the office.

After some time, Hawkins finally emerged. He slammed the door and pitched a five-hit shutout. Williams just smiled at his postgame news conference.

Chris Welsh Incident

Chris Welsh is currently a successful commentator on Cincinnati Reds TV. Whenever the Reds are in San Diego, we usually laugh about an incident in 1983, when Chris played for the Padres.

Welsh was a left-handed pitcher making his first start of the season. Chris had blanked the Pirates for two innings, but in the third, Pittsburgh had runners on first and third with one out. Lee Mazzilli was the batter.

Dick Williams had a standing rule for his pitchers with runners on first and third: "Don't throw to first base." Williams didn't want the runner to score from third on a mistake, such as a balk or wild throw. Welsh was aware of the manager's rule. Twice, he threw to first base.

Williams sent pitching coach Norm Sherry to the mound to discuss the situation. Norm reminded him, "Chris, you know the rule. Don't throw to first in this situation."

Welsh responded, "Well, I'm going to . . . the longer I make Mazzilli wait at the plate, the better chance I have of getting him out."

"It doesn't matter," said Sherry. "Those are Dick's orders."

"Well, I'm going to throw to first again, and you can tell Dick that," replied Welsh.

"Chris, do you really want me to tell Williams that?" pleaded Sherry.

"Yes," said Welsh firmly.

Norm passed the response to Williams, who phoned the bullpen. Welsh finished the inning and then was removed from the game.

The next day, Chris was a Montreal Expo.

I Never Forget My Little League Signs

Eric Show is the Padres' all-time leader in pitching wins. Show won 100 games during his San Diego career, eight more than Randy Jones.

I found Eric a fun guy to be around. He would argue with anybody about any subject without getting belligerent. He had many interests, including music. Several times, I returned to the Grand Hyatt Hotel in New York late at night to see Show playing the piano in the lobby.

However, sometimes Eric could be exasperating to his manager and pitching coach.

Norm Sherry remembers one such incident. Show was batting with a runner at third base and one out. Eric was a decent hitter, and Dick Williams decided to let him swing the bat. Dick notified third base coach Ozzie Virgil, who immediately went through a myriad of signs. None of them meant anything. Show was on his own to hit. He took a fast ball right down the middle.

Williams groaned but decided to let Show hit again. After more meaningless signs from Virgil, Show took another fastball down the middle for strike two. Williams walked away muttering as Show struck out on the next pitch.

Sherry approached Eric in the dugout. "Eric, did Virgil give you a sign?"

"He most definitely did," said Show.

"What sign did he give you?" wondered Sherry.

"He crossed his chest, then went straight down like a 'T'—that's the take sign. . . ." Show replied. "Oh my gosh, that was my take sign in Little League!"

The San Diego Chicken

The original San Diego Chicken was the KGB Chicken and was manned by diminutive college student Ted Giannoulas, who was

Everyone's favorite fowl, the San Diego Chicken.
From the San Diego Hall of Champions Collection

hired by KGB Radio to wear the suit for promotional functions around the city. Ted definitely deserves all the credit for taking the job to a higher level. He merely adlibbed his way around San Diego Stadium—no skits were prepared in the beginning. He particularly enjoyed the coeds in the bleachers, though. It's amazing what you can get away with while wearing a chicken suit. Ted's off-the-wall antics caught the city's attention, and soon, the Chicken became a San Diego sensation and eventually the most famous poultry in America.

One time, Ted almost created an international incident. When the touring Russian National Hockey Team came to the San Diego Sports Arena to play the local minor league team, some high-level diplomacy was required to convince the Russians that the "KGB" Chicken wasn't mocking the Russian secret police.

Inevitably, Ted would outgrow the KGB job. A dispute arose between Ted and the radio station. Eventually, a judge ruled that Ted could wear a chicken suit, but it would have to be different from his KGB suit. Andy Strasberg, creative Padres marketing director at the time, arranged for the chicken to unveil his new outfit prior to a baseball game—it turned into an unbelievable show.

Chicken Re-Hatches

Exactly 41,822 showed up at San Diego Stadium on June 29, 1979, to watch the Padres host the Astros—and to witness the re-hatching of the San Diego Chicken. The pre-event publicity had been amazing.

Strasberg arranged for a huge Styrofoam egg to be on display above the right field wall to help generate interest. Several days before the big event, some college kids stole the egg as a prank. Along with all the local newscasts, I always suspected that Strasberg had arranged the heist to intensify interest.

"I wish I had been that smart," commented Andy. "But it really was just a prank by the students."

The kidnappers ended up negotiating a safe return of the egg through a TV news anchor, which generated even more publicity. The criminals had to be college students, because the egg was released for a ransom of two cases of beer.

The day before the re-hatching, the egg was on the field for a news conference. Maybe it was a slow news day, but many members of the media showed up. To this day, I remember newscasters holding microphones up to the Styrofoam egg to interview Ted Giannoulas, who was inside.

What great video. . . .

Finally the big day arrived. Strasberg arranged for the egg to be placed atop a Brinks armored truck and escorted into the stadium by motorcycle police. The theme song from *2001: A Space Odyssey* blared over the public address system.

The Brinks truck stopped between third base and home plate. Several Padre players carefully removed the egg and placed it on the ground. Following a short pause, the egg started rolling around the infield. Then Ted kicked his way through the Styrofoam and emerged to a huge roar. Padre players Kurt Bevacqua and John D'Acquisto lifted the chicken on their shoulders and marched around the diamond.

Strasberg remembered, "A note came over the wire service stating Padres-Astros game delayed due to grand hatching of chicken."

Who Cares About a No-Hitter?

Five years later, Strasberg and the Padres held an anniversary party to celebrate the rebirth of the chicken. 45,468 fans showed up for the fun and got more than they bargained for.

There were many chicken bits, but the biggest was saved for the seventh inning. The Padres were hosting the St. Louis Cardinals, and Strasberg arranged for two actors to wear Cardinal uniforms. The chicken began making fun of the Cardinals in front of their dugout. The actors started to chase him. The chicken jumped into the stands and raced toward the scoreboard where the make-believe Cardinal players cornered him.

The chicken was supposed to jump from the 18-foot high wall onto a mattress hidden behind the eight-foot inner fence. "In rehearsal, Ted wouldn't jump because he was afraid of heights," recalled Strasberg. "But when he put the chicken suit on, he had no problem jumping."

So the chicken leaped to elude the fast-closing "Cardinals." The fans thought the bit was over.

Not over. . . .

After a brief pause, the chicken emerged from the right field corner riding a horse while *Indiana Jones* music pulsated over the PA system. The idea was for Ted to ride the horse to the left field corner. Unfortunately, the horse spooked and stopped dead in center field. "My heart stopped," Andy said. "But in reality the game was delayed for only 30 seconds."

There was another more serious problem. Cardinals hurler Ricky Horton was pitching a no-hitter. Did the chicken act have an effect on him? We'll never know, but Kevin McReynolds ended his no-hit bid with an eighth-inning double. Horton still achieved a two-hit 5-0 shutout win.

Where's The Leak?

Bill Posedel was the Padres' pitching coach in 1974. Bill began his baseball career in 1929 and finally made it to the major leagues with Brooklyn in 1938. He retired as an active player after the 1947 season with a lifetime record of 41-43.

Posedel served in the Navy from 1942-1945, earning the nickname "Sailor Bill."

He worked as pitching coach for the Oakland A's from 1968-73 and is credited with developing pitchers like Vida Blue and Jim "Catfish" Hunter.

Posedel had no pitchers with that kind of talent on the 1974 Padres. He often told me it was the worst major league pitching staff he had ever seen.

"Sailor Bill" loved to go out for dinner. On many occasions, I joined Bill, fellow coaches Jim Davenport and Jack Bloomfield, and manager John McNamara.

Posedel was 67 years old, but he still loved to pull his favorite prank in restaurants. He would dip a spoon into his glass of water and launch the liquid toward an unsuspecting table. He would then quickly look up at the ceiling and hold his hand out like there was a leak. Occasionally, he would repeat the trick multiple times and enjoyed it more when people at the adjoining table would call for the manager concerning the "leak" in the ceiling.

Only once did I see Bill get caught red-handed. He laughed and picked up the other party's dinner check.

Whitey Wietelmann

I first saw Whitey Wietelmann play baseball when he was a short-stop for the 1949 Padres at Lane Field. It was an association with San Diego baseball that lasted nearly half a century.

Whitey began his pro baseball career in 1937 at Beaver Falls, Pennsylvania. He was an excellent defensive shortstop, and the Boston Braves called him up to the majors in 1939. The Braves manager was Casey Stengel, who asked the young shortstop his name.

"Billy Wietelmann," he responded.

"From now on, it's Whitey," Stengel told him.

"I had platinum blond hair then," Whitey recalled. "That's been my nickname ever since."

The baseball commissioner, Judge Kenesaw Mountain Landis had issued a directive not to play rookies against first-division clubs. Stengel ignored the directive and started Wietelmann and rookie second baseman Sibby Sisti at Wrigley Field against the Cubs. Both Whitey and Sisti played well, and the Braves won the game. Landis was at Wrigley Field and directed the two rookies to approach his box.

"I was shaking in my shoes," Whitey admitted.

"Congratulations, boys, I think I made a mistake. You can play," Landis told them.

"That may have been the greatest thrill I ever had," recalled Whitey.

I Already Did!

Wietelmann could certainly handle pain. While pitching batting practice for the Braves, a line drive hit him on the hand, which nearly severed the tip of his little finger. A tourniquet was quickly applied to stop the bleeding, and two doctors were summoned as Whitey sat in the training room. The doctors examined Wietelmann and then huddled to decide what to do. Finally, they told Whitey they had decided to cut the finger off.

"I already did, Doc," said Whitey, holding a pair of scissors.

Jim Thorpe and Cy Young

In 1925, when Wietelmann was six years old, he was the batboy on a Zanesville, Ohio semi-prefessional team managed by his dad. On that team was an outfielder named Jim Thorpe—arguably one of the greatest athletes in American history. Thorpe was a terrific football player at tiny Carlisle College and won several track & field gold medals in the Olympics. Like Michael Jordan, Thorpe found baseball more difficult to play. In six major league seasons, Thorpe hit only seven home runs and batted .252.

A retired baseball pitcher named Cy Young lived near the small Ohio town where Wietelmann was raised. Young won 511 games during his major league career and was nicknamed Cy because he threw the ball like a cyclone. Whitey was the only other major league player in the area, and Cy Young loved to have him come for a visit and talk baseball.

Whitey told me he once asked Young the secret of his success. According to Wietelmann, Young said it was his legs. Cy never picked up a baseball in the off-season, but he would run constantly to strengthen his legs. Young told Whitey he could then pick up a baseball and throw it as hard as he wanted.

Phil Collier

I considered Phil Collier one of my best friends. We shared a love of baseball and golf. Many others also thought highly of Collier. In 1990, he was selected for the writer's wing of the Baseball Hall of Fame in Cooperstown, New York. Phil was president of the Baseball Writer's Association of America in 1979. In the mid-1990s, the press box at Qualcomm Stadium was named after him.

Why all this adulation?

Phil Collier came to San Diego from Fort Worth, Texas, in 1953, and covered the PCL Padres for the *San Diego Union*. When the Dodgers moved from Brooklyn to Los Angeles in 1958, he was assigned to the major league baseball beat. The Los Angeles Angels were born in 1961, and Phil covered both teams depending on which club was home. I always thought his baseball writing in those days was as good as it gets.

Beginning in 1969, Collier switched to covering the major league Padres. Club president Buzzie Bavasi credited Phil's writing with creating an atmosphere in San Diego that helped the city acquire major league baseball.

I've never known a media reporter who had as many inside baseball contacts as Phil Collier. He established such rapport and trust with Dodgers great Sandy Koufax that the Hall of Fame pitcher phoned Phil the day before his retirement announcement so Collier could break the national story in the *San Diego Union*.

My Friend, Sandy Koufax

Speaking of Koufax, Phil loved to tell stories. The Dodgers had two excellent relief pitchers in Bob Miller and Ron Perranoski. The pair was used frequently by manager Walter Alston. When Koufax

Ray Kroc and Phil Collier. From the San Diego Hall of Champions Collection

was scheduled to pitch, they figured that they wouldn't have to work—so they'd enjoy a night on the town. One night, Koufax was having a rough outing, and Alston went to the mound. Miller and Perranoski were laboring in the bullpen. Alston asked Sandy, "How are you feeling?"

"Skip," Koufax responded. "I'm not feeling too good, but I know I feel better than those two guys warming up in the bullpen." Koufax finished the game.

Times Change

In the '70s and '80s, Phil had to receive permission from his bosses at the newspaper to do a pregame radio interview. I always felt the interview would only enhance Collier's standing with his readers. He would suddenly become a recognizable voice when people saw his by-line in the morning paper. He certainly wasn't going to give me a scoop before writing it in his own story. How times have changed.

Catcher Chris Cannizzaro was the Padres' first All-Star. "Occasionally, after a tough game behind the plate, I would call Collier in his room," Chris told me. "He always invited me over for a drink, and we would talk well into the night. It was the only way I could relax enough to get to sleep. I don't think Phil ever intentionally hurt a player in print, which is one reason he got so many good stories."

"What About Your Spare Time?"

During Collier's days of covering major league baseball, he never took a game off. Not only did he cover the game, he was hired by the league to serve as official scorer when the Padres were home. This entailed extra time after writing his story to fill out the official scoring sheet and send it to Major League Baseball. Phil also was paid by the Padres to keep the team's statistics and type them on a mimeograph for the next day's game. Eventually I assumed this responsibility, and it took me about two hours to compute, type, and record all the stats. In addition to all this, Collier wrote a weekly story for *The Sporting News* and was the San Diego baseball stringer for *Sports Illustrated*. I'm not sure what he did in his spare time—if he had any.

Phil loved to partake in a cocktail or two. He often told me his autobiography would be entitled, *The Bases were Loaded—And So Was I*. Unfortunately, Collier didn't finish this book before cancer took him at the age of 75.

Tim Flannery

Tim Flannery has always been one of my favorites. When he was a player he never gave less than 100 percent, which endeared him to the fans. When he was a coach, he was always available for an interview and provided valuable inside information to the broadcasters. Now he's working hard to become the best broadcaster he can be. There are two Flannery stories I especially love to tell.

Hero to Goat

In the mid-1970s, Flannery was a 10th grader on his Anaheim High School baseball team. In a key playoff game, Anaheim was facing a tough Santa Ana Valley High team led by Garry Templeton.

The score was tied in the 12th inning when Flannery doubled. Tim was sacrificed to third and scored the winning run on a sacrifice fly. His teammates hoisted the young sophomore onto their shoulders and carried him off the field in celebration. However, Santa Ana appealed the play. Their claim was that Flannery had left third base too soon. The umpire agreed, and the game remained tied.

The Anaheim players immediately dropped Flannery to the ground. . . . Plunk!

Who's That Mascot?

In 1993, Tim Flannery was a first-year manager of the Padres Spokane club in the rookie Northwest League. Spokane was facing Billingham in a playoff game when there was a violent collision at home plate. Flannery and his Spokane players thought it was an unnecessary cheap shot. The benches emptied, and the umpires warned both teams. Flannery told his pitcher not to retaliate . . . justice would come later.

Instead, the pitcher promptly drilled the next Billingham batter. The pitcher and Flannery were immediately ejected from the game.

Flannery sat in the clubhouse listening to the game on the radio when the team mascot came in for a break. Flan described the mascot outfit as a cross between a dinosaur and an anteater, which I will leave to your imagination. Either way, Flannery informed the dinosaur anteater that his day was over. Flan commandeered the outfit.

Venturing onto the field as the mascot, he tried not to draw attention. All of a sudden, the music started, and Flannery was dancing on the field to "Louie, Louie."

Coming off the field, Tim passed his wife, Donna, and said, "Hi, Honey." One can just imagine what Donna thought.

Sidling up to the Spokane dugout, he started issuing orders to the players—quickly commanding them not to give away his disguise. Flannery could just envision a major suspension if the umpires discovered he was on the field in a mascot costume. It was probably the first time the young Spokane players had ever taken orders from a mascot. Alas, Spokane lost the game, but Flannery's disguise remained a secret.

Chapter 16

Tony Gwynn Bits and Pieces

Wait Until Basketball Season Ends

In view of Tony Gwynn's Hall of Fame career, it's hard to imagine that every team in baseball had two cracks at the eight-time batting champion before the Padres selected him in the third round of the 1981 draft. Padres General Manager Jack McKeon always surmised that, because Gwynn was a star on the San Diego State basketball team who reported late for baseball, many scouts missed him.

The Aztecs had a tremendous shortstop at the time named Bobby Meacham, who eventually was drafted in the first round by St. Louis. Many scouts saw Meacham and the Aztecs early in the season, but few were aware of Tony when McKeon visited Montezuma Mesa after basketball season. Jack liked Meacham but was enamored with Gwynn. He wanted to draft Gwynn in the second round, but his scouts talked him out of it. They preferred a pitcher named Bill Long, as in the long-forgotten Bill Long. Jack relented, but insisted that Tony would be his next pick.

Fortunately for the Padres, he was still available.

Gwynn's Debut

Padres fans eagerly anticipated the arrival of Tony Gwynn in the major leagues. Based on his basketball and baseball exploits at San Diego State, Tony was already a well-known San Diego sports figure.

When he became the Padres' third-round draft choice in June 1981, his minor-league accomplishments garnered unprecedented interest.

Gwynn led the Rookie Northwest League with a .331 batting average and was selected league MVP that first summer of 1981. Anticipation increased when he moved up to Double-A Amarillo in the Texas League for the final three weeks of the season and hit .462 in 91 at-bats. In 1982, a little more than a year after signing his professional contract, Gwynn was batting .328 for the Padres Triple-A affiliate in Hawaii when his call to the major leagues came.

Tony arrived in San Diego on July 19, 1982, and was immediately inserted into the starting lineup by manager Dick Williams. The former collegian played in center field and was batting fifth in the order against the Philadelphia Phillies.

In his first at-bat, Gwynn hit a sacrifice fly to center field, scoring Tim Flannery from third. Tony lined out to shortstop in his second at-bat and struck out in his third. In the eighth inning, though, Gwynn collected the first of his 3,141 hits—a double to left field. In the last inning, Tony rapped out his second base hit, a clean single, which brought a rousing ovation from the 34,433 in attendance, sensing something special about this debut.

As the young hitter stood on first base, acknowledging the cheers, Phillies first baseman Pete Rose offered his congratulations. "Nice going, but don't try to catch me in hits in one night!" Baseball's all-time hit leader could obviously spot talent.

The 22-year-old Gwynn would bat .289 in 54 games that year—his only season in the majors under .300.

A Valuable Dick Williams Lesson

Tony learned a valuable lesson in July 1984.

"I hit a routine double-play grounder to second base and didn't run hard to first. Ron Oester bobbled the ball but was still able to turn the double play. Dick Williams immediately took me out of the lineup and put Bobby Brown in right field. Later in the game Brown messed up a fly ball, and we lost."

When Williams called him into his office the next day, Tony was upset about being removed from the game. The manager asked, "Do you know why I took you out of yesterday's game?"

San Diego's beloved eight-time batting champion Tony Gwynn (1984).
From the San Diego Hall of Champions Collection

Tony answered that he did.

"You know you cost us the game," snarled Dick.

"How did I cost us the game?" Gwynn responded. "You took me out."

"Because I had to put Brown in right field," Williams snapped back. "And he messed up a play. If you had been out there you'd have caught the ball."

.400 in 1994?

Would Tony Gwynn have batted above .400 had the 1994 season been played to its conclusion? It's a question that will never be answered. We do know that Gwynn was hitting .394 when major league baseball came to a halt on August 11 due to a labor dispute. We do know that Gwynn had hit safely in the last 14 games he had started. We also know Tony was batting .475 during his previous 10 games (19 for 40).

What does Tony Gwynn think?

"I would have hit .400," Tony states emphatically. "That year I wasn't being fooled. I wasn't swinging and missing. I wasn't chasing pitches. If that year had continued, I would've hit .400 . . . there is no doubt in my mind."

I also believe Gwynn would have hit .400 that season. Not only was he "in the zone" as a hitter, but his ability to deal with the media would have helped him. He wouldn't have been affected by the daily postgame press conferences or the speculation surrounding each at-bat.

Most Satisfying Batting Title

"1988 was my most satisfying batting title," opined Tony Gwynn. "I won the title with a .313 average, the lowest winning average in the history of the National League." The previous low mark was .320 by Larry Doyle of the 1915 New York Giants.

Tony underwent hand surgery during spring training and suffered a knee injury that put him on the disabled list in May. Yet Gwynn did not mention those injuries as the reasons for his hitting problems that resulted in a .237 average in June and a .246 mark on July 2.

"I simply couldn't stay back," remembered Tony. "I was out in front with my swing, and I had real doubts about the season."

What turned it around for Gwynn?

"I was facing Bob Walk of Pittsburgh, and he threw me a back-door slider. I stayed back on the pitch and lined a single to left. I thought to myself, that hit might turn around my season."

Tony went on an 18-game hitting streak and batted .406 for the month of July. In his last 73 games, he averaged .367 and ended up winning the third of his eight batting titles by four percentage points.

Gwynn also led the 1988 Padres in hits (163), RBIs (70), and stolen bases (26).

A Lost Batting Title

Nobody in the history of the National League has won more batting titles than Tony Gwynn. Gwynn and the legendary Honus Wagner—each captured eight crowns.

"It's nice to be even with Wagner, but it would be even better to be above him," said Jerry Coleman and Tony's dad, Charles Gwynn, Sr.

Gwynn was well on his way to winning the title in 1991 when torn cartilage in his left knee made it difficult for him to play. A .425 batting average during May and June lifted Tony's average to a robust .373, and he was voted a starter for the All-Star game. Watching him daily during the second half of the season, it was obvious to observers that the bad knee was affecting his play.

Many people were urging Gwynn to have immediate surgery on the knee. "My dad and Jerry Coleman were on me every day to take care of my knee, but I didn't want to win a batting title that way," remembered Tony. "I guess Jack Clark was still in my head, and I didn't want to be perceived as selfish."

Gwynn batted just .243 after the All-Star break and finished with a .317 average. Terry Pendleton won the title with a .319 mark.

Tony eventually had arthroscopic surgery on his left knee to smooth out the cartilage.

Best Season

Tony Gwynn won his eighth and last batting title in 1997. In his opinion, he saved the best for last.

"It was my most complete season," stated Gwynn. Statistically, it was a magnificent year. Tony batted a major league-high .372 with personal bests in home runs (17), RBIs (119), hits (220), and doubles (49).

Two years earlier, Gwynn was visiting Ted Williams at his Hitters Hall of Fame museum in Florida. Ted told Tony, "History is made on the inside pitch." He urged Gwynn to turn on that ball and drive it. Gwynn argued that he wasn't really that kind of hitter, and the conversation ended.

In 1997, Tony decided to give Williams's suggestion a try.

"In late June, I hit three home runs over a four-game span by turning on the inside pitch and driving it over the wall," remembered Gwynn. "From that time on, I noticed pitchers stopped throwing inside to me, and I was able to hit the ball all over. Finally, I understood what Ted meant."

Williams and Gwynn were both at a postseason banquet following the 1997 season, and Tony publicly acknowledged the advice he received from Ted. I asked Tony what Williams did.

"He winked at me," said Gwynn.

Almost Hitting for the Cycle

Matt Kemp (2015) and Will Myers (2017) became the first Padres to hit for the cycle—a single, double, triple, and home run in the same game. On June 10, 1993, Tony Gwynn came very close.

It was a home game against the Dodgers, and Gwynn homered in the third inning. In the fifth, he doubled to left center. In the sixth, he tripled to right. All Tony needed was a single. Who has a better chance to hit a single than Gwynn? The Padres were leading 11-2, and manager Jim Riggleman removed Tony from the game.

Did Tony mention to Riggleman that all he needed was a single to hit for the cycle?

"No," replied Gwynn, "and Rigs was really upset at me after the game when he found out . . . but I still had Jack Clark in my head and didn't want to be perceived as being selfish, thinking too much about myself . . . plus, I always thought another opportunity would present itself."

It never did.

Yankee Stadium

In 1998, the Padres defeated Houston and Atlanta in the playoffs to win the National League pennant.

"It was after the last game in Atlanta, I knew we were going to Yankee Stadium," recalled Gwynn. "And I had never been there. It was one of my final goals in baseball."

The next day, most of the players took the subway to Yankee Stadium for the traditional pre-World Series workout.

"I had my son, Anthony, with me," Gwynn said. "When we entered the stadium, there were signs to the locker room and the monuments. We immediately headed for the monuments. There was such a feeling of history as I took pictures of the famous monuments—players like Ruth, Gehrig, DiMaggio and others."

Prior to Game 1 of the series, Gwynn was chatting with announcer Keith Olbermann. "I told him it's going to be awesome to hear legendary Yankee P.A. Announcer Bob Shepherd say my name."

Tony did not know that Shepherd was standing right behind him. The P.A. man intoned, "How would like me to introduce you? Would you prefer Tony or Anthony?"

A startled Gwynn turned around. "Oh, Mr. Shepherd, I don't care. Whatever you call me, it'll sound great."

After the World Series ended, Tony was pleasantly surprised to receive a gift from Olbermann. "He sent me a charm, and when you press a button, you hear Bob Shepherd announcing my name. I have that charm in my special trophy case."

Three of the four games between the Padres and Yankees were very competitive, but a superior Yankees team won in four straight. Gwynn remained appreciateive. "Even though we lost in four straight, the experience of playing in Yankee Stadium was just great."

Tony's Final Game

October 7, 2001, was Tony Gwynn's final game. What does Tony remember most about it?

"It sucked . . . that game really sucked. Your last game you should play, and I couldn't . . . my knee wouldn't allow it."

I wondered if he considered starting in right field, batting in the first inning and then coming out of the game?

"I did," said Tony, "But I didn't trust myself that I could handle a fly ball hit to right field."

What about before the game?

"I actually took extra hitting with Rickey Henderson and Phil Nevin, trying to spray the ball to all fields. When we were done hitting, I took a long, slow walk around the stadium."

Bruce Bochy asked Gwynn when he wanted to hit.

Tony Gwynn. From the San Diego Hall of Champions Collection

"I told him late in the game, and it turned out to be the ninth inning when we were trailing Colorado 14-5. What I wanted to do was get a hit between third and short (the 5.5 hole). I knew the pitcher would throw me a fastball, and he did. Unfortunately, I was just a little anxious and hit a one-hopper to the shortstop. To me, that was the end. The ceremonies were great, but after that last at bat, it was over."

Epilogue

Hall of Fame for Gwynn

"Validation" is the way Tony Gwynn described his election to Baseball's Hall of Fame—validation for a wonderful 20-year career with the Padres that included eight National League batting titles, yet only 135 career home runs. Thinking about his late father, Charles, Tony broke into tears when the official phone call came.

"It's the first time I've ever seen him cry," noted Gwynn's wife, Alicia.

Nearly 98 percent (97.6) of the 545 voting baseball writers wrote Gwynn's name on their ballots. Seventy-five percent is required for induction. Tony's percentage is the ninth highest percentage in Hall of Fame history. Pitcher Mariano Rivera received the highest vote percentage, 100, in 2019—the only player to ever be unanimously inducted into the Hall.

Gwynn's reaction was typical Tony: "I'm really happy the way things worked out. I really didn't want to set any all-time induction record."

Since 1945, only Ted Williams's .344 lifetime batting average exceeded Gwynn's career .338. When Tony visits the Hall of Fame, he will notice the size and quality of gloves from the early twentieth century. Back then, gloves barely covered a player's hand. Modern gloves rob hitters with great catches in the outfield and superb stops in the infield. With his style of hitting, I believe that Gwynn's lifetime average would be significantly higher had he played in an earlier era.

Tony's Hall of Fame career started in the backyard of his childhood home. He and his brothers would make balls from rolled socks wrapped with rubber bands. They hit them with a broom-handle bat. No doubt his hand-eye coordination and bat control benefited from those early makeshift games.

Following his career with the Padres, Tony became the baseball coach at San Diego State, his alma mater (the Aztec team plays on campus at Tony Gwynn Stadium). The Gwynn baseball legend at San Diego State began in 1981, after he concluded his basketball career with 16 points and 16 assists in a season-ending victory over New Mexico. The following day, Tony appeared in an Aztec baseball uniform and, without any practice, went 6-for-9 in a doubleheader.

Tony's emotions started to show the day before his election was announced. When baseball practice concluded, his players started chanting "Hall of Fame." During ceremonies at Petco Park the next day, the entire Aztec baseball team showed up in matching black jerseys. They sang the Aztecs fight song as Gwynn left the podium. It was another tearful moment for Tony.

"I was a good player," noted Gwynn, "but I knew my place. I was not a game-changer. I was not a dominant player."

Sorry, Tony, I have to disagree. You were a dominant player, just not a dominant player who hit home runs.

Fortunately, Tony lived to see a Tony Gwynn statue erected beyond the center field fence at Petco Park and enjoy his induction into the Baseball Hall of Fame on July 29, 2007. The San Diego icon and Padres greatest player passed away on June 16, 2014, after battling cancer.

"Hells Bells"

In 1992, Gary Sheffield became the only Padre aside from Tony Gwynn to win a batting title. Sheffield was a strong candidate to capture baseball's Triple Crown that year before a late-season injury ended his dream. A fan favorite, Sheff was sent packing to Florida as part of the infamous 1993 Padres "fire sale." Fans were discouraged, but this five player deal did bring a promising but unknown young set-up pitcher to San Diego. His name: Trevor Hoffman.

When Hoffman became a free agent at the end of the 2005 season, the Padres almost lost him to Cleveland. At the last minute, Trevor reportedly agreed to stay for less money than the Indians were willing to pay. All year, the club marketed his pursuit of Lee Smith's all-time career saves record. On September 24, 2006, in the Padres' final home game of the season, Hoffy sent the Pittsburgh Pirates down in order to register save No. 479, breaking Smith's record. The last man Hoffman faced that day was National League batting champion Freddy Sanchez.

One can argue the validity and evolution of the save as a significant baseball statistic, but if a team does not have a pitcher who can consistently slam the door in the ninth inning, that team will not be a winner.

During his major league career, Trevor has been successful in nearly 90 percent of his save situations, the best mark in baseball history.

I asked Bochy about managing without Hoffman in the bullpen. "Oh man, was I lucky to have him in San Diego. There's no doubt I've been spoiled." In 2006, Trevor led the National League with 46

Trevor Hoffman celebrates after recording save No. 479, making him the all-time saves leader.
from the San Diego Padres; Chris Hardy, team photographer

saves, while finishing the season with a stellar 2.14 ERA. The former Padres manager revealed that, "Trevor was bothered after blowing a save in the All-Star Game, and it affected him for a short while." Two of his five blown saves for the year came in the week after the ASG. Other than that, Bochy said, "He had his usual year, and there's no reason he can't continue to be successful."

Hoffy was successful enough to finish with a National League record 601 saves. He had his number 51 retired by the Padres in 2011, was elected to the Padres Hall of Fame in 2014, and was inducted into the National Baseball Hall of Fame in July 2018. The next month a statue of Trevor was unveiled at Petco Park, joining other Padres heroes Tony Gwynn and Jerry Coleman. Major League Baseball now officially names the National League Fireman of the year award after Trevor Hoffman. The American League Award is named after Mariano Rivera.

Bruce Bochy

When this book initially came out in hardcover, the first chapter covered the 2005 championship season. While discussing that campaign with Bruce Bochy last year, I mentioned that I had just played golf with four guys who had all been fired as major league managers: Roger Craig (by the Padres), Norm Sherry (by the Angels), Bob Skinner (by the Phillies), and Alan Trammell (by the Tigers). At the time, Bruce replied, "I'll tell you one thing, Bob. I'm never playing golf with you." As I began my interview about the 2006 season, Bochy started to laugh. "Now maybe I can play golf with you guys."

Bochy was not fired after the 2006 season, but had been told he would not receive a contract extension. He was free to talk to several other teams about open managerial jobs. What had Bochy done to deserve this treatment? For the first time in club history, he guided the Padres to consecutive division titles. He did it with teams that very few baseball people had picked to win. Significantly, Bochy earned nearly $2 million a year . . . more than Padre management wanted to pay.

Contrary to some reports, Bruce wanted to continue managing the Padres. He was unsure why management took this stance, but didn't ask. Instead, Bochy signed a lucrative three-year contract to manage the San Francisco Giants with a commitment from owner Peter McGowan to spend whatever it takes to reach the World Series.

McGowan was true to his word, and Bochy managed the Giants to World Series victories in 2010, 2012, and 2014.

Qualcomm to Petco—Nothing but the Facts

The Padres played 35 seasons at San Diego/Jack Murphy/ Qualcomm Stadium. They began as a major league expansion team in 1969. It took the Padres 10 years to record their first winning season (84-78) in 1978. During their time in Mission Valley, they only managed nine winning seasons, but captured three division titles and reached the World Series twice.

In 1984, the Padres overcame a two-game deficit in the league championship series with a three-game sweep of the Chicago Cubs in San Diego, only to lose, four games to one, to a powerful Detroit Tigers team in the World Series.

In 1998, the Padres breezed to the NL West title, then defeated Houston and Atlanta in hard fought playoffs to face the New York Yankees in the World Series. Many long time baseball observers felt the '98 Yankees were the greatest New York team of all time. The Yankees didn't disappoint, sweeping the Padres in four games, although three of the games were close.

The Padres also won the division in 1996 by sweeping Los Angeles the final three games of the season at Dodgers Stadium. However, the St Louis Cardinals swept them in a three game playoff series.

On to Petco in 2004

Through the first eight seasons at Petco Park, the Padres competed for the division title five times, winning it twice in 2005 and 2006. The '05 team took control of the division by winning 22 of 28 games in May and coasted to an NL West title. They were swept in the playoffs by St. Louis, the only club to win 100 games that year. The '06 Padres also lost to the Cardinals in the postseason and St. Louis went on to win the World Series.

In 2007, the Padres and Colorado Rockies tied for the wild card, one game behind division flag winner Arizona. The clubs met in a

Former Dodgers teammates Roger Craig, Johnny Podres and Al "The Bull" Ferrara were all part of the original San Diego Padres in 1969.

one-game playoff with Colorado capturing a wild 9-8, 13-inning affair. The Rockies eventually reached the World Series, only to be swept by the Boston Red Sox.

The 2010 Padres surprised the experts by leading the NLWest for most of the year. As late as August 25, the Padres enjoyed a 6½-game lead. Unfortunately, a 10 game losing streak cut the Padre lead. They still led by ½-game with eight contests remaining, but fell three games behind the Giants facing a season-ending three-game series in San Francisco. The Padres kept their title hopes alive by winning the first two games, but the Giants prevailed on the final day to win the division. On a roll, the pitching-rich Giants went on to capture the 2010 World Series.

The Petco Park Controversy

Eric Judson was a former UCSD baseball player who advanced within the Padres organization to vice president of Ballpark Development. He worked closely with former Padres President Larry Lucchino in all facets of Petco Park construction including the out-field dimensions.

Judson explained, "We wanted to reward pitching and defense at Petco, a philosophy emphasized by Lucchino." The Padres conducted wind pattern studies at the site to help determine the outfield dimensions. "We wanted a fair ballpark" said Judson, "but if we erred, we wanted it to be on the side of pitching and defense. We also felt with the distance of the outfield gaps, there would be more triples, which is one of the most exciting plays in baseball."

The Padres achieved the desired result—Petco Park is considered one of the best pitching parks in all of baseball.

During the Padres last years at Qualcomm Stadium, their two best power hitters were Ryan Klesko and Phil Nevin. From 2000-2003, Klesko hit 26, 30, 29, and 21 home runs. His two seasons at Petco resulted in 9 and 18 homers.

From 1999-2001, Nevin hit 24, 31 and 41 home runs at Qualcomm. Injuries limited him to 25 homers in the last two years. An outspoken critic of the Petco dimensions, Nevin still hit 26 home runs in 2004, but the following year, while playing only 73 games, his production dropped to nine home runs. Nevin had great power to

Petco Park. From the San Diego Padres

right centerfield, but right center is Death Valley at Petco. Potential home runs die in outfielders gloves.

In 2004, Padres General Manager Kevin Towers quipped that Petco was built to be "Barry Bonds-proof." Bonds called it "baseball-proof."

In my view, power is the most expensive and difficult commodity to find in baseball. It's far more cost effective for the San Diego market to build contending teams through pitching and defense.

The Team of the Military

The San Diego Padres are recognized throughout professional sports as "The Team of the Military." In 1995, the club established a Military Affairs department headed by Navy Captain Jack Ensch. The former prisoner of war and executive officer of the Navy's "Top Gun" school established close ties with the local military community.

Rear Admiral James J. "J. J." Quinn, current head of the Padres Military Affairs office, continues the team's ongoing commitment to our armed forces.

For Sunday home games, the Padres wear camouflage uniforms. The Marine Corps Hymn is played in the fourth inning and soon-to-graduate-boots and their drill instructors from Marine Corps Recruit Depot watch the game from high in the right field stands. In addition, rotating members from all branches of our armed forces sing "God Bless America" during the seventh inning stretch over the PA system during these Sunday home games.

An informal tradition dates back to the Pacific Coast League era when young sailors and marines flocked under very different circumstances to watch baseball at San Diego's largest saloon: Lane Field. In the old days, vendors didn't check IDs very closely.

Later, Marines attended Sunday games in Mission Valley under the watchful eyes of their drill sergeants, and alcohol was not consumed.

Today, the Padres sponsor "Military Appreciation Day," "Salute to Veterans," "POW/MIA Recognition Day," "Military Spouse Appreciation Day," and "Military Opening Day," among other special events.

Pacific Coast League Heritage

In 1936, the Pacific Coast League Hollywood Stars moved to San Diego and were renamed the Padres. When the National League expanded in 1968, PCL Padres owner C. Arnholt Smith purchased a major league franchise for the 1969 season.

Over the years, the Padres have honored their PCL roots by keeping their name and the Swinging Friar mascot.

There is a bronze bust of Johnny Ritchey at Petco Park. A year after Jackie Robinson broke the color barrier in the major leagues, Ritchey broke the Pacific Coast League color barrier in 1948 when he played for his hometown Padres.

Another native son, Manuel Hernandez, is honored with a display inside the Padres "Salute to the Military" exhibit at Petco Park. Hernandez played for the Padres in 1944 and was drafted into the Army and killed in action in 1945. He is the only Padre to have made the supreme sacrifice for his country.

There is an exhibit at the Padres Hall of Fame Plaza that includes a plaque for every former Padres player who entered the National Baseball Hall of Fame, including Ted Williams, Bobby Doerr, Bob Lemon, Larry Doby, and Tony Perez who played for the Coast League team. In 2016, Ted Williams was also inducted into the Padres Hall of Fame. The Hall at Petco Park traces the history of baseball in San Diego, including the PCL and the major league Padres.

2016 MLB All-Star Game

Retiring commissioner Bud Selig awarded San Diego its third All-Star Game for 2016. During his "farewell tour" visit in 2015 to San Diego, the Padres unveiled the "*Selig* Hall of Fame at Petco Park," which drew immediate and widespread criticism.

Two weeks before the 2016 All-Star Game, the new *Padres* Hall of Fame opened at Petco Park. Sports columnist Nick Canepa wrote, "It wouldn't have mattered if Bud's name was on a sprinkler head in the outfield. It wasn't a good idea [to name the Hall of Fame after him]."

Special brown and yellow commemorative jerseys were worn for All-Star Workout Day and the Home Run Derby.

The body of the National League jersey was brown with yellow raglan sleeves. The American League design was reversed with yellow body and brown raglan sleeves. Team logos were on the left sleeve and right side of the commemorative caps. The jersey and cap script was stylized 1980s Padres lowercase.

The American League won the game, 4-2, and Kansas City Royals first baseman Eric Hosmer was named MVP for his two-run homer in the second inning and RBI single in the third. In 2018, Hosmer joined the Padres.

Bob's Personal Observations About the All-Time Padre Players:

Seventy-five years of Padres baseball—dating back to the original Pacific Coast League team in 1936—were celebrated in 2011. In 2012, I gave my observations about the all-time team as selected by veteran *San Diego Union-Tribune* sportswriter Bill Center and San Diego baseball historian Bill Swank.

Perhaps as an indication of the Padres lack success since 2010, the all-time team stays pretty much intact. However, that could change dramatically in the next few years. The arrival of 20-year-old shortstop Fernando Tatis Jr., during the 2019 season is the main reason. In my view, he has more raw talent than any player in Padres history, and barring injury should be the top shortstop for many years to come.

In 2019, the Padres also signed third baseman Manny Machado to a massive 10-year, $300 million contract. Some feel that, despite a subpar 2019 season for Machado, he still hit 32 home runs, displayed gold glove ability at third base, and could end up as the Padres best all-time player at that position.

Catcher

BENITO SANTIAGO is the most talented catcher to play for the Padres. He broke in with a bang as the unanimous NL Rookie of the Year in his first full season of 1987. All he did was catch 146 games, bat .300, hit 18 homers with 79 RBIs, steal 21 bases, and set a club record that still stands by hitting in 34 consecutive games. He dazzled observers with his strong arm and especially enjoyed throwing out runners from his knees. Benito had soft hands and a wiry build.

Watching him during his first few years, I honestly thought he was headed for the Hall of Fame. But stuff happens. By 1993, he was gone from San Diego. He continued to play many more years in the majors, but never came close to matching his early productivity.

TERRY KENNEDY was the first building block of the 1984 NL Champion Padres. GM Jack McKeon engineered an 11-player trade with his old buddy Whitey Herzog in St. Louis. The Padres gave up Rollie Fingers, Gene Tenace, Bob Shirley, and Bob Geren to acquire Kennedy. McKeon made the deal because he wanted a young power-hitting catcher. Terry was selected on three NL All Star teams and batted .295 with 42 doubles, 21 homers, and 97 RBIs in 1982. Although he never achieved those numbers again, he was the catcher on the Padres first World Series team in 1984 and remained the number one receiver until the arrival of Benito Santiago.

First Base

ADRIAN GONZALEZ is hands down the best all-around first baseman in Padre history. The only thing he didn't do well was run. I've never seen a first baseman charge a bunt and get the lead runner at third base as well as Adrian. He probably ranks among the top half dozen players in baseball. In my view, one of the unfortunate aspects of baseball is that only a few teams can afford a player of Gonzalez's caliber, who signed a contract with Boston paying him over $20 million a year.

NATE COLBERT was the Padres first star position player. He took over first base during the expansion Padres first season and immediately established himself as one of the game's premier power hitters. In both 1970 and 1972, he hit 38 home runs while playing at San Diego Stadium—when home runs had to clear an 18-foot high outfield fence. On August 1, 1972, he hit 5 homers with 13 RBIs during a doubleheader in Atlanta. He also drove in 111 runs in 1972, a remarkable achievement since the team scored a total of only 488 runs the entire season.

Second Base

ROBERTO ALOMAR is in baseball's Hall of Fame. He is by far the best second baseman to ever play for the Padres. He was only

Nate Colbert. From the San Diego Padres

20 years old in 1988 when I first saw him in Yuma, Arizona, during spring training. His range, hands, and arm were outstanding, and he could already turn a double play with the best in the game. He was the complete package.

I'll never forget my disappointment when General Manager Joe McIlvaine traded Alomar and Joe Carter to Toronto for shortstop Tony Fernandez and first baseman Fred McGriff. McIlvaine's comment was, "I'd rather have a great shortstop than a great second baseman." Padre fans were deprived of watching a Hall of Famer for the next 10 years.

Two other Padre second baseman deserve recognition. ALAN WIGGINS was a speedy outfielder who switched to second base in 1984. Wiggy was a key factor in San Diego's first pennant, batting leadoff and stealing 70 bases. He was such a threat to run that number two hitter Tony Gwynn won his first batting title with a .351 average.

With Wiggins in high gear, Gwynn received a high dose of fastballs. Tony batted .412 when Wiggins was on first base.

MARK LORETTA also deserves special mention for his incredible 2004 season at Petco Park. Mark was a smart and savvy player who batted .335 with 208 hits. He scored 108 runs with 47 doubles, 16 homers, 76 RBIs, 16 sacrifice flies, and a .391 on base percentage. It was one of the best all around seasons ever by a Padre player.

Third Base

In 1998, KEN CAMINITI had arguably the greatest individual single season in Padres history. Cammy was the National League's unanimous MVP after batting .326 with 40 home runs and 130 RBIs. He homered in the All-Star game and won a Gold Glove for his defensive brilliance. His diving, backhanded stop of a grounder and throw from a prone position won the ESPY for baseball that year. Caminiti also played the entire season with a torn rotator cuff in his left shoulder. His locker was located next to the training room entrance. Many times I witnessed players about to enter for treatment, but turn away after looking at Caminiti, who persevered in pain.

GRAIG NETTLES deserves honorable mention. Near the end of a terrific career, he was acquired from the New York Yankees at the conclusion of spring training in 1984. He proved to be the final piece in the Padres first World Series run. Nettles supplied 20 homers, 65 RBIs, superb defense, and veteran leadership for a predominantly young team.

Shortstop

OZZIE SMITH and GARRY TEMPLETON are the two top shortstops in Padres history and, ironically, they were traded for each other.

In 1978, Padre Manager Alvin Dark observed Ozzie Smith playing in the Arizona Winter League and immediately recognized the defensive talent that would eventually land Smith in the Hall of Fame. Ozzie had an excellent season, finishing runner-up to Bob Horner for NL Rookie of the Year. Early that year, Ozzie made a defensive gem that still qualifies as his signature play. Against Atlanta at San Diego Stadium, the Braves Jeff Burroughs hit a hot shot up the middle. Ozzie dove to his left for the ball, but it hit something and bounced erratically. In mid-dive, the acrobatic shortstop reached back and grabbed the ball with his bare hand. He quickly jumped to his feet and threw the surprised Burroughs out at first.

Although Smith continued to field brilliantly through 1981, he batted only .230, .211, and .222 his last three seasons in San Diego. When a contract squabble developed prior to the 1982 campaign, the Padres traded him to St. Louis for Garry Templeton (who was considered to be a much better offensive player). Tempy served as the starting shortstop until the early '90s and anchored the San Diego infield during the 1984 pennant run. He was credited with igniting the crowd in game three of the playoffs against the Cubs in San Diego. Templeton also contributed a key defensive play to stop a Chicago first inning threat and added an important RBI double later in the San Diego victory. The Padres won the next two games to reach the World Series.

Outfield

TONY GWYNN is not only one of the best Padre outfielders of all time, he is by far the greatest all-around player in Padres history. You know a player is special when he is mentioned in the same conversation as immortals like Honus Wagner and Ty Cobb. Gwynn and Wagner each won eight batting titles, the most in National League history. Ty Cobb is the only player with more batting crowns (12). There's much more on Gwynn in chapter 16 of this book.

DAVE WINFIELD became the first player to enter Baseball's Hall of Fame as a Padre.

Winfield was the Padres first draft choice out of the University of Minnesota in June 1974. After signing with San Diego, Winfield asked scout Donnie Williams whether the Padres wanted him to pitch or play outfield. Williams responded, "Big boy, we want you to swing that bat every day." Winfield did, never playing an inning of minor league baseball.

STEVE FINLEY is my choice as the Padres best all-around centerfielder. In 1996, he finished among the top five in MVP balloting while Ken Caminiti was the unanimous winner. All Finley did was play in 161 games, bat .298, score 126 runs, collect 195 hits with 45 doubles, 9 triples, 30 home runs, 95 RBIs, steal 22 stolen bases, and earn a Gold Glove for defense in center field.

Special mention is also deserving of CITO GASTON and GREG VAUGHN. Gaston was the Padres' original centerfielder. He was an excellent outfielder with a strong arm who hit .318 in 1970 with 29 homers and 93 RBIs. Vaughn was a key member of the 1998 pennant winning Padres and the only San Diego player to hit 50 home runs in a single season.

Starting Pitchers

Lefthander RANDY JONES lost 22 games in 1974 and became one of the best pitchers in baseball during the 1975 and 1976 seasons. Randy won the NL ERA title in '75 and the Cy Young award in '76. He became so popular in San Diego each section of fans would stand and applaud as he walked to the left field bullpen to warm up. When he was finished and headed for the dugout, the fans would stand and applaud again. There's much more on Randy Jones in chapter five.

In 1998, KEVIN BROWN had the most dominant single season of any Padre right-hander. He was acquired from the Florida Marlins in a deal for future All-Star first baseman Derrek Lee and only pitched one season in San Diego, but what a season it was. Brown was arguably the best NL starter in 1998 as he led the Padres into the World Series against a powerful New York Yankees team. Kevin started 35 games for San Diego with an 18-7 record and 2.38 ERA while pitching 257 innings and striking out 257 batters. He won two more games in the playoffs and had a 5-2 lead against the Yankees in the seventh inning of Game One during the World Series. Unfortunately for the Padres, illness forced Brown from the game and the Yankees roughed up the San Diego bullpen to win.

GAYLORD PERRY won the Cy Young Award for the Padres in 1978. He was 21-6 with a 2.73 ERA. He turned 40 in September and devoted his Cy Young Award to all the 40-year-olds in the country.

JAKE PEAVY was another San Diego Cy Young winner. Peavy won the honor in 2007 with a 19-6 record, 2.54 ERA and 240 strikeouts in 223 innings. Unlike Brown and Perry, Peavy was a product of the Padres farm system, arriving in the majors in 2002. I'll never forget his debut. He had just turned 21 when he faced the New York

Yankees in front of 60,021 fans at Qualcomm Stadium. Despite losing 1-0, he gave a glimpse of good things to come with a three-hit performance that had the Yankees singing his praise.

ERIC SHOW was another product of the San Diego farm system. He came up in 1981 and pitched for the Padres through the 1990 season. Three times he won 15 or more games and his 100 all-time victories are still tops for a Padres pitcher.

Relief Pitchers

TREVOR HOFFMAN heads the list of an impressive group of Padre closers. The Padres acquired him in 1993 from the Florida Marlins for slugger Gary Sheffield. He pitched for the Padres through 2007. Along the way, he became baseball's all-time saves leader and now ranks second to the Yankees' Mariano Rivera. In 2011, Hoffy had his Padres number 51 retired and he seems guaranteed to soon enter Baseball's Hall of Fame.

ROLLIE FINGERS is in the Hall of Fame. He was signed as a free agent prior to the 1977 season and saved over 100 games before being traded to St. Louis in the Terry Kennedy deal. His 37 saves in 1978 set a NL record at the time. Fingers saved 11 of Gaylord Perry's 21 victories. It was a different era for closers, as Rollie would pitch up to four innings to save wins.

GOOSE GOSSAGE is another Hall of Famer who would frequently pitch two or three innings to record a save. The fire-balling Gossage signed as a free agent with the Padres in 1984 and helped pitch San Diego to its first ever World Series.

Lefthander MARK DAVIS deserves special mention. In 1989, Davis won the Cy Young when he saved 44 games with an ERA of 1.85.

Adding to a long list of impressive Padres closers, KIRBY YATES turned in 41 saves for a 70-win Padres team in 2019, and deserves to join this elite list.